The Software Engineer's Guide to Corporate Survival

"You're not actually afraid of the thing itself; you're afraid of failure. Don't be!"

- The best advice my dad ever gave me.
Thanks Keith Pulsipher!

the Software Engineer's

Guide To

CORPORATE

SURVIVAL

```
// crack the code to thrive
// in a big company
sellYourSoul = false;
```

Jon Pulsipher

ISBN-13: 979-8-88-496440-2

Contents

More advance praise for *The Software Engineer's Guide To Corporate Survival…*

"**I wish I had this book months ago.** It would have saved me a lot of time and frustration. So much of my education was focused on technical skills, but few resources touched on the unspoken rules of business- until now. This book feels like grabbing a coffee with an industry expert. Grateful for the confidence-boost and the corporate roadmap. The advice here has made me a more well-rounded developer."
 - Derek Askham
Software Engineer

"After 37 years in the industry, I have developed the tools for myself that has allowed me to work effectively with my co-workers, managers and leadership teams to achieve success as a software engineer. **If I had the information in this book, I could've easily shaved 10 years off my journey.** The five pillar approach to building your career helps simplify and clarify what things you should focus on so that you can stand on the shoulders of those before and not have to re-invent the wheel."
- Karl Hilsmann
Principle Software Engineer
Microsoft

"Jon has an incredible knack for cutting through the jungle of occupational nuance and ambiguity to clearly explain theoretically simple but practically complex concepts. It's not that these topics are completely foreign to the average reader, but **he teaches them so well that it will make you say, 'Wait, why wasn't I doing this before?'** An excellent resource at any point in your career."
- Cody Byers
Data Engineer

Foreword

When Jon first mentioned that he was writing about corporate survival for software engineers, I felt a mix of curiosity, concern, and excitement. Curiosity stemming from Jon's wealth of interesting and varied experiences, from which I knew he could offer profound insights; concern about the provocative title "corporate survival," given our industry's tendency to veer towards cynicism; and lastly, excitement because I trust Jon to strike the right balance on this delicate and nuanced topic. And indeed, he has.

In the pages that follow, you will engage in an honest conversation with an industry expert. Jon articulates his principles for survival and connects them to his own experiences in a direct, thought-provoking, and even humorous manner. From "Knowing your job" to "Don't be annoying," Jon touches on all those messages I've tried to share with other engineers throughout my corporate experience and brings them into sharp focus. Whether you're a seasoned corporate survivor or a corporate rookie, this book will offer dozens of real-world experiences that will compel you to reflect and apply these insights to your own career.

The Software Engineer's Guide to Corporate Survival offers an engaging alternative to dry discourses on corporate culture. With candor, humor, and honesty, Jon shares numerous stories that kept me chuckling and nodding in recognition. He then masterfully transforms these shared experiences into thought-provoking discussions that can be applied to your life.

Beyond the principles, Jon offers valuable insights on your overall career journey, emphasizing the importance of communication and collaboration to achieve consensus, and even touches on the impact of AI. He encourages you to be an engaged, productive team member and provides advice on handling challenges. Each chapter prepares newcomers for what to expect and prompts veterans to consider how the advice could be applied to their current situations.

Whether you are just stepping into the corporate world as a software engineer or you're a veteran seeking inspiration, dive into this book. You're guaranteed to come away better equipped, possibly a bit wiser, and much more prepared to navigate the corporate environments we encounter.

Enjoy the journey,

David Markley
Vice President of Technology

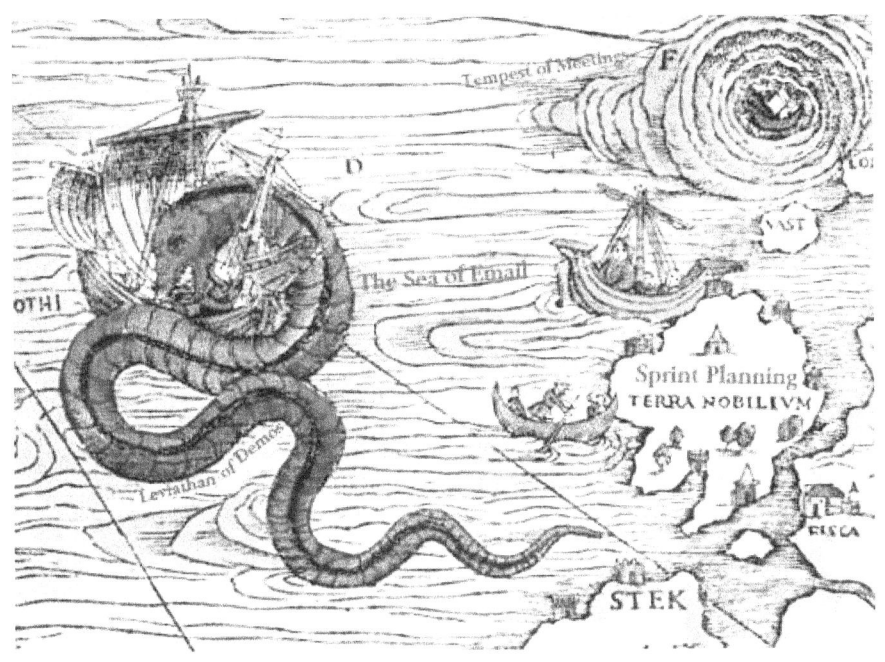

Introduction

Why I wrote this book

In 1994, I worked for the US subsidiary of a small British company doing consumer mapping and route planning software. This was before broad consumer availability of GPS and way before Google Maps on a smartphone. Our US team had about a dozen employees and the parent company wasn't much larger, maybe 20 people. Late in that year, we were acquired by our much larger nearby neighbor – Microsoft, which at the time was about 31,000 people. Honestly, many of us were terrified just due to the unknowns of it all. It turned out to be a great thing for the business and for us personally. Our products turned into the now long-gone Microsoft Automap and MapPoint and several of us contributed to Encarta Encyclopedia and Encarta World Atlas, and, over time, Microsoft Office, SQL Server and Xbox.

Fast forward to that difficult COVID-19 year of 2020. I was working at Unity Technologies, the maker of one of the preeminent game engines in the world. Unity acquired a small

European company with a great product and a team of less than 20 people. In this case, several of those people had worked together on this product for well more than a decade – and some had literally never had any other job in software. These are smart, driven engineers, designers and managers, and they were deeply tied to their customers. Unity had about 6000 people at the time, small for me after Microsoft and Amazon, but almost incomprehensibly huge for these folks. And just for fun, let's remember it was during a global pandemic when travel was limited and they were on another continent, not just down the road. I found myself manager, mentor and counselor-in-chief to this team as it navigated multiple culture clashes and a firehose of change. I felt lucky to be able to draw on my own previous experiences, not just in 1994 but in other teams and groups who were navigating strong currents of change. I helped teams work through this at Twitch, after it was acquired by Amazon, and a small speech recognition company as it courted a variety of suitors, as well as seemingly countless teams within Microsoft, Amazon and Unity experiencing such significant reorganizations that it seemed as though they had been acquired by a larger entity. The collected successes, failures and lessons learned over all those experiences seemed worth writing down. Not just for people whose whole company has been acquired by a larger one, but for the person who previously worked in a small organization and has now moved to a big one, or even those navigating the changes that come with internal consolidations and re-organizations – the apparent national sport of technology companies.

A note about terminology

I'll use the word "company" frequently. I try to balance it with "organization" and other such words, but I am treating all of these as synonyms. An organization or company is the top-level entity you work for. It could be a public or private company like Microsoft Corporation, it could be a non-profit organization like United Way, or it could be a governmental institution like the United States Treasury Department, or even a church. All of those, like all companies, have their own structures, rules, and norms and they all employ software engineers.

Going down below that top level, within any kind of organization there are smaller units of some kind. These may be called subsidiaries, regions, departments, divisions, product units, and many other names all the way down to something you might call a team, a pod, feature team or scrum team. These generally have at least most of the same policies that are dictated by the company as a whole, but they may have additional rules associated to a geographic region or type of customer. For example, a business unit inside a larger company that deals with medical devices or one that deals with government customers, will have very specific policy requirements related to those special regulatory environments. And, just because it happens with any group of people, they will almost certainly have their own norms, behaviors and idiosyncrasies. Generally, I refer to all of these as "teams," though I do cycle through synonyms just for better reading.

Essentially, there are "big entities" that we'll usually call "companies" and "small entities" we'll usually call "teams." Try to find your own specific situation in the use of those terms.

Another thing to be aware of is that in some companies, they will call you a "software engineer" and in others they will call you a "software developer." Sometimes, this is just culture, habit and preference. Other times it can actually reflect a legal requirement. In some countries, the title "engineer" can only be used for licensed or otherwise regulated jobs – like an electrical engineer or civil engineer – and software engineering doesn't meet that kind of licensure bar. As someone who has worked mostly in the United States, I tend to use the term "software engineer" but it really isn't that important.

What this book is and isn't
Right up front, this book is *not* about the daily work of developing software. There is nothing in here about how to design systems, write code, define APIs or use frameworks. You won't find how to run a daily scrum meeting or how to manage a backlog or any of that; there's a lot written to help you do that part of your job. There are great Substacks, blogs, books, podcasts and conferences. By the way, one of my favorite books in this area is *The Pragmatic Programmer* by David Thomas and Andrew Hunt. If you haven't read it, you should add it to your reading list – but finish this one first. This book is about how to do that *other* part of your job. The part about managing your career, making sense of complex organizational challenges and dealing better with all the things that get in your way while you are trying to do the part of your job that relates to code. In a lot of ways, these other problems are more complicated. There is no auto-complete and no compiler warnings to help you deal with finding your place inside a large company or in communicating with all the other people involved in your projects.

Every organization, even those of the same size, is somewhat unique. We're engineers; we find comfort in structure and process; we'd all really like a checklist with the exact steps. Unfortunately, this can't be that, *but* in this book I've provided guidance that, while a bit generalized, comes from my own experience as a software engineering team member and leader in some notable companies, as well as hundreds of hours of interviews with dozens of other technology leaders and influencers from a wide variety of organizations and backgrounds.

While there is no universal magic plan you can follow exactly, there's certainly nothing here that is harmful. I would hope you have, or can build, a relationship with your manager, and perhaps other people you can trust, to fill in any specific details for your specific situation and organization.

I'll also give the caveat that I've spent my career in technology companies that work primarily on mass market products and services. There are definite cultural differences that come along with that business. If you are working in a heavily consulting oriented company or if your team serves internal customers and stakeholders, those teams sometimes have cultures and "rules" that are unique and different. (Such as the need to maximize billable hours and to continuously "sell yourself" internally to stay on the best active projects.)

As you read on, you'll see that I make some generalizations about software engineers. Like any labeling, you may look at yourself or people you know and agree or disagree with certain of those. These are simply based on traits I have seen in myself and in other developers over decades. People are complicated and it's impossible to accurately describe all of our individual personalities in a few words, so please accept these as just some broad buckets of tendencies, rather than simple stereotypes.

Why you need this book

You're a good engineer. Maybe even a great one.

You can code like crazy and deliver high-quality and well-architected features and solutions to customers. That is enough to thrive, right? Why do you need a book like this? These are natural questions.

Won't your good work stand out and be recognized on its own merits?

Unfortunately, the answer to that is, at best, "not really." Doing the work, and doing it well, is just the beginning. Even in organizations with a strong engineering culture, doing excellent work by itself is just not enough to give the best odds for continuing to thrive and have additional opportunities. There is more to the equation, and this book is to help you build up additional tools to not only do great work but be viewed as someone who does great work.

I've seen, and I suspect you have too, capable software developers, even primary subject matter experts on key systems, passed over for raises and promotions, left out of hot new projects, not given the respect they seem due, or perhaps even seemingly cast aside in layoffs.

What, then, makes the difference? What's the secret?

There is a common belief that to successfully advance your career you need to manage people. I'm not here to tell you that message. I have worked as a senior individual contributor and as a people manager, and in roles that mix the two, but I know that managing people is not something everyone wants to do. Even if they have previously been successful managers or leaders, they may have decided that's not for them. That is 100% fine!

If you don't feel drawn to manage teams, then you definitely should **not** do it.

Regardless of other skills, a person who finds themselves managing people when they don't want to do that is simply not going to take that craft seriously and they won't be good at it. This not only harms that person, but the people working under them. It's a big responsibility.

If you are in a people management role and it just isn't for you, please have that conversation with your own manager. Don't just stick with it. That road won't lead to a good place.

If for some reason you find yourself in an organization that requires people management as part of the growth path, and your heart doesn't take you that direction, then for everyone's good you should start looking for other opportunities that provide growth *without* requiring you to manage people you don't want to manage. Thankfully, the idea that you must become a manager to grow your software engineering career is becoming much less common.

"Become a manager" is **NOT** the message of this book.

This book is also not a screed or manifesto against large companies or corporations. I've spent some of my happiest and most productive years at Microsoft and Amazon, as well as smaller companies. Every group of people is going to have its own dynamic. Since these relational dynamics occur even in very small organizations (even in a family), to condemn that is as effective as shouting against a hurricane.

So "big companies are evil" is **NOT** the message of this book. Who has influence? Who makes things happen – or stops them?

The surprise is that it isn't necessarily the people with titles like "Chief _____" or "Director of _____."

Many teams have strong influencers – the *connectors*, *salesmen*, and *mavens* as Malcom Gladwell referred to in *The Tipping Point*. Not everyone is going to be one of those types. This book isn't about convincing you to become one. There is a deep relationship to personality and you sort of have it or you don't.

"Become a connector/salesman/maven" is **NOT** the message of this book.

BUT if you aren't one of those types of people, that doesn't mean you can't and shouldn't build a relationship with someone who is and think about how you can become a valuable part of *their* networks.

Most importantly, know you aren't alone. At risk of stereotyping a bit, a lot of engineers tend to immerse themselves in the work and are happy not to engage deeply with other people in the ways that will be good and necessary for them to reach their full potential. This book is your map to what might seem like an uncharted land of where you can both be productive **and** achieve career success.

Small versus large

There's a lot to be said for working in small companies. Often there is a shared sense of purpose and camaraderie, an energy, a hunger and, often, but not always, some amazingly

9

innovative ideas. A small group of people can get together and pour their heart and soul into a common effort and really do great things. The bond that comes from that environment often leads to a deep sense of trust and familiarity between people that approaches the ability to read each other's minds. So, given all that, why work anywhere else?

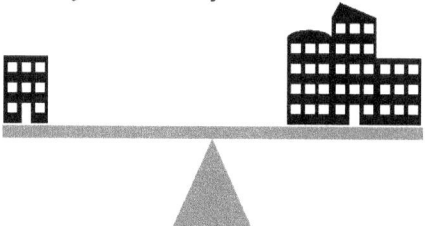

Small organizations tend to develop a few particular classes of problems:

- **Scaling their product and their market.**
  Many small companies have a single "big idea" and a single product. That lack of diversification is a risk, even if that one product is great. If you have a business that can reasonably support, for example, six developers, a couple salespeople and a couple support/overhead positions, the universe of value you can deliver to customers is limited by that size. Your ability to experiment beyond things that satisfy immediate customers' needs is limited. Everyone is already busy rowing the boat you have.
- **Executing against large deals.**
  As you move into larger deals, those customers will have expectations around security certification, Service Level Agreements (SLAs), specific liability insurance and more. All of these things have their own costs. Robert Matyszewksi referred to this in his blog post "Advantages and Problems of Small Software Company" (https://softwarehut.com/blog/it-outsourcing/advantages-and-problems-of-small-software-company) as "The Glass Ceiling" for small companies. The paradox is that your ability to secure

the deals you need to grow your company may be out of your reach because you are a small company.

- **Money stuff.**
  Finally, the money. Whether it is cash flow or ability to attract investment, small companies can struggle with money. And that means they may struggle with competitive compensation, which gets in the way of attracting more top talent. The counterpoint to this is that as long as the small company can avoid desperation, these struggles can sharpen focus and drive innovation. These very struggles can, as your grandfather might say, "build character."

- **Becoming rigid.**
  I can hear you asking, "What? Isn't that a big company problem?" It can be, but even small companies can lose that important "start-up mentality." Sometimes this is brought on by fear or desperation setting in among the leadership team. This often causes these small, agile teams to become just as inflexible and slow to react as some large companies can be. In a small company where you find this affliction, it can actually be even more dangerous and hard to change just because there are fewer projects going on and fewer people bringing new ideas into the organization.

There's another small-company tendency that came up repeatedly in my interviews with engineers who have experience in both small and large companies. It doesn't rise to the general level of those I just listed, but it seems important to note. In some small companies, you will often hear the message that "we're a family" or "we're all in this together!" but whether intentionally or not, these slogans are really an appeal to a sense of belonging that is used to drive team members to work harder and longer, and when things go badly, some of those "family members" are suddenly no longer part of the family.

Often, working in a larger organization mitigates, at least somewhat, all of those problems – and substitutes different ones.

- **Bureaucracy and silos.**
  Larger more established companies do bring with them larger and more established bureaucracy – and sometimes this sets in when the company isn't even really that large. Along with that institutional friction, territorialism can develop that gets in the way of solving broader customer problems and which take a lot of leadership and willpower to break through.
- **Money…again.**
  Organizations that are publicly traded or which have significant private investment also need to satisfy the demands of those investors. Where money goes, control surely follows. Also, within a large company you might be part of a smaller organization. Perhaps working on a new product that is an area of investment rather than revenue. Cost centers can attract a different kind of scrutiny than profit centers and can essentially have similar financial struggles to those of a small company standing on its own.
- **Distance from the customer.**
  As organizations scale, the tendency is for the distance between the customer and the developers and other team members delivering the product to grow. The development team starts to see feedback as something that is delivered in highlights and summaries from marketing, product management or other functions. They may begin to see satisfaction measured as a score rather than as direct conversations and reactions. This doesn't *have* to be this way, but it takes effort to overcome the tendency.

Working at a large company can open the door for software engineers to work on investigational projects that don't immediately turn into revenue and, generally speaking, provide at least a tacitly greater level of employment security, opportunity and compensation.

Again, there are exceptions, and as we look around to our friends, colleagues and perhaps even ourselves, we've all seen that "job security" anywhere is really an illusion. Adding to all this, many large companies struggle with *The Innovator's Dilemma* challenges that Clayton Christensen captured so well.

You might sum this up with the saying that, generally at least, small companies have lots of ideas and energy but less ability to execute, while big companies have more money and the ability to do things but sometimes can't figure out the right way to use those advantages.

As you can see from this discussion, there is no definitive criteria that says one is always better than the other. Often, though, one opportunity is better for *you* at a specific *point in time*. When comparing any two roles, you really have to think about which takes you from the place you are now to a better place in your career and personal development five years from now. That isn't always the one with the highest salary today.

This book is focused on helping software engineers in those large companies, but most of the information that follows will also help you achieve your best in smaller ones too.

Let's put some pros and cons in a table so we can compare small and large companies. These are generalities, of course. If you are considering moving between these two worlds, you might build on this with the specifics of the companies you are choosing between.

	Pros	Cons
Small	**Flexibility:** Small companies often have more flexible work environments and more flexibility in assignments and projects. **Visibility:** You may have more visibility and opportunities to take on diverse roles. **More Team Cohesion:** Smaller teams often lead to closer collaboration and stronger relationships.	**Limited Resources:** Small companies may have limited resources for training and development. **Stability:** There might be higher instability and risk compared to larger, more established companies. **Limited Benefits:** Smaller companies may offer fewer benefits compared to larger counterparts.
Large	**Resources:** Large companies usually have more resources for training and professional development. **Stability:** Larger companies tend to have a stronger financial footing, which gives them the opportunity to experiment and invest in new ideas. **Benefits:** Larger companies tend to offer more comprehensive benefits packages. **Résumé enhancing:** There is something to be said for having the right, recognizable names on your résumé.	**Bureaucracy:** Large organizations may have more bureaucratic processes. **Less Visibility:** You might have less visibility, and it could be challenging to stand out. **Specialization:** Larger companies may require more specialized roles, limiting your scope of work. **Coasting:** There is a greater chance in larger organization for non-productive or non-engaged employees to be "hiding out" and just receiving a paycheck.

Principles of Corporate Survival

It seems almost a legal requirement that you can't have a career book without distilling the message down to some set of principles. I can't fight against that law, so here are the Five Principles of Corporate Survival for software engineers. The rest of this book is organized around these tenets.

1) **Nail your job.** Before you can focus on anything else, you need to be good-to-exceptional at the basics of your job. Usually that means designing good solutions; delivering solid, tested code; and doing what you commit to do.

2) **Make a map.** Be familiar with (but don't try to memorize) the org chart. Understand who has *power* and who has *influence* and the difference between those two things. Know the rules of your organizational culture and how to stay off the Human Resources (HR) naughty list.

3) **Know the business.** You don't need to be a product manager or the CTO, but you should have at least basic answers to these questions:
    - Who's the customer?

- What's the vision or overall direction? How your work and that of your team aligns with it?
- What does success look like for the organization?

4) **Manage your own brand.** No matter what, you will be known as some kind of person – that's your "brand." Accept that truth and, without going to Kardashian™ level, manage it at least a little bit.

5) **Don't be annoying.** Help ensure other people will cooperate with what you are trying to do. Think about how you will handle making a mistake yourself or when someone else does. Know when to listen and when to speak.

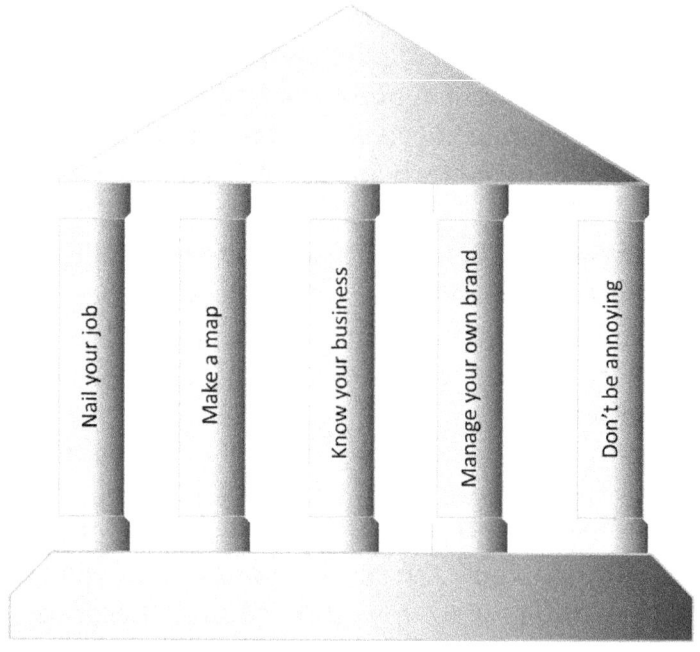

Let's start our journey by diving into each of these principles in detail identifying a set of action steps that we can start taking right away.

Principle #1: Nail your job

It probably goes without saying, but the first step is to get a handle on the basics of your job. Headcount is precious and you were hired to do....*something in particular.* As soon as you are hired and complete the immediate sort of human resources new-hire tasks, you need to start very quickly to show progress on learning and doing your core job.

For the rest of the book, I'm going to cover a lot that may not seem directly related to software engineering. None of that will help you if you can't do the basics of your job of building and delivering software that fits the needs of your team, company and customers.

Like any craftsman, you can't do your job if you don't know your tools. When I say "tools," I mean that in the broadest sense. Not just specific software you use, but also frameworks, workflows and processes.

Understand the technologies involved, the other systems you need to connect with, and whatever tools your team uses in their work. Maybe your team uses Atlassian Jira® to track work items, Microsoft Visual Studio Code as your editor and

GitHub for version control. Bare minimum, you need to be able to see the work assigned to you, write the code to build a new feature or fix a bug, and do a local build to test your changes.

Every team uses some way to track who is doing what and when. Maybe it is Jira, Azure™ Boards, Smartsheet™, sticky notes on a whiteboard, whatever. You really need to know that tool and pay attention to it. No one wants to drop any ball. However, if someone had asked you to do something in a casual hallway conversation, and you forgot about it, that's definitely an easier conversation than if you just didn't do something that was documented and assigned to you in the place your team's work normally lives.

I've worked with a surprising number of developers over the years who needed to be reminded to look at the work assigned to them, or even how to do it. Don't be that person. If the tool or system is unfamiliar to you, ask for help. You don't need to know every detail of it, but you need to know how to find your work and the workflow steps you need to perform to move the work along the way to completion.

If you are new to the job

Most teams have an on-boarding process or a designated "buddy" to help you come up to speed. Pay attention to this. You definitely do not want to be known as the person who isn't able to do much. You also need to understand *how* your team is delivering work. What software methodology do you use?

As an example, let's say your team uses Scrum. You'll obviously want to know how long your sprints are, where to find your backlog, and how your team handles planning and estimation. What does a release mean for your team and how often does it happen?

You are going to ask a lot of questions in this phase. There's no way around that and that's fine. However, when you care enough to ask a question and someone cares enough to answer it, then you should care enough to remember (or better, to write down) the answer. From time to time, we all ask questions we have asked before, but doing this too much will lead to an early reputation as someone who doesn't pay attention to the answers or advice.

Your manager or team may or may not set specific goals for you in terms of expectations for your first 30, 60 and 90 days. Even if they don't, you should set some personal goals for that timeframe and consider discussing them with your manager. This initial time on the job, sometimes called the "honeymoon period," gives you a chance to learn a lot and understand what you need to do to be productive. It's also a time where you are setting the first impression your new team will have of you. Invest some effort to stretch yourself here. This is almost always a time when people are the most tolerant of new people asking questions. Don't be afraid to play that "new guy card." I would balance that with the need to resist the urge to say things like "At my last company we did it this other way and it was much better." For now, be more a seeker of information. Ask more than tell. Listen more than talk. There will be a time for driving change later when you have a good feel for personalities and sensitivities.

As you ask these questions and gather this information, it is a good time to find, or make for yourself, information about the systems you work on – text descriptions, data flow diagrams, block diagrams, data models, etc. Things that allow you to confirm your understanding of how things work. Some of this will flow naturally from the discussions you are having with others on the team and that provides a good opportunity to check your understanding of what they are describing on the spot and correct it if needed. You might find that an hour of valuable discussion can be boiled down to one or two basic diagrams.

If you are further along in the role

If you are reading this while you are in a role that you've been in for a while, that's great too. Take some time before you move forward with the other principles to do a personal assessment on whether you are nailing the basics of your main job. To do this, you need to have a clear idea of what "good" looks like. Talk to co-workers who seem to, well, be doing a good job. Look for people that others respect and listen to. Check the places your organization stores information – documents on shared drives, SharePoint®, Wikis, intranet, Slack, etc. – for "job architecture" or "career ladder." If your company has a designated training coordinator or team, often part of Human Resources, ask them. Finally, don't ignore the most basic step of looking back at the job description for the job you have. There isn't always enough detail or clarity in a job description, but take a look.

You should also think about previous discussions, and perhaps annual reviews, you've had with your managers over time, even in other roles or teams. What feedback have they offered? If you really look at it objectively, do you see truth in it? Are there action steps they've suggested that you haven't done?

If you have solid friends who can give you honest feedback on personal and professional characteristics, ask them for their thoughts.

If you feel you have some work to do there, invest in that. Talk to your manager, observe other team members who are viewed as strong contributors on the team and perhaps even talk to your manager about your plan to fill in any gaps in your understanding.

For everyone

The best advice I can give you for this principle is to be a person who does what they say they will do. I recall at the

Microsoft New Employee Orientation I attended many years ago, the executive guest speaker said, "We are an entire company built on the idea that people will do what they say they will do." He went on to say that if a person took on a task, it was just expected they would do it. If they dropped the ball and didn't tell anyone they were blocked or needed help or had some conflict, it could literally be too late to do anything about it by the time other people found out it wasn't going to happen. This seems crazy, but it worked. The culture of the company at that time was so tuned around that behavior that it was exceedingly rare that someone just failed to deliver without saying anything ahead of time. People had a true ownership mentality and would do anything they could possibly do to make sure they delivered their assigned pieces.

If you commit to something, do it. If you don't feel like you can truly commit to something, then raise that objection early. Make sure you state the reason and be open to help with whatever is in the way. "I can't deliver this feature in a week because I've never worked in this system at all. Is there someone with more experience that could support me on that?" or "I can't take this on because I have these other tasks that are higher priority. Am I right about the prioritization?" This approach signals that you are open to it, but you need help overcoming what seem to be obstacles.

If the unexpected happens, whether it is a technical issue or something involving other people or teams, speak up about it. The sooner the better. It will look better for you if you also suggest some course of action rather than just saying you're stuck and don't know what to do. If you are stuck and you don't know how to fix it, saying that is still better than not saying anything.

Some of this discussion of taking on tasks and when to push back on taking on more things will be covered in more detail later in, in the *Beyond the Essentials* section of the book.

Managing your time

To really deliver on your commitments, you have to learn to manage your time effectively. That doesn't mean making a habit of working crazy long hours, skipping lunch and working weekends. Yes, there are particularly busy times that require more of our time now and then, like when you are launching a new system into production, when you need to make a delivery that is aligned to an unmovable calendar date such as a holiday, or when you are one part of a multi-faceted effort that is all coming together to a single product. In fact, on a highly functioning team, there's a certain energy and excitement that can come from these periods. What you definitely can't do is make a high level of crunch a routine and accepted part of your life and your schedule. It's not sustainable professionally or personally and you will end up suffering from that path.

What's the alternative then? Learn to better control your time. OK, managing your time is easier said than done, yes, I agree. Still, there are techniques you can use.

- **Don't pretend it isn't an issue for you.** Everything we do in this business is ultimately driven by the clock and calendar. Even if you are estimating tasks purely in story points, which are intended to indicate relative complexity and not task time, eventually someone asks a question like "Can you have this done by May 10th?" Maybe they aren't asking you personally. Maybe they are asking your lead or your project manager, but *someone* is going to be asked that question. Part of that conversation should include, if push comes to shove on an unmovable date, what *could* you deliver by that time? What else could move around? Engage in the discussion, don't just say it can't be done.
- **Control what you can control.** There are a lot of things you can't control or at least not fully. You can't control when people schedule meetings that disrupt your

productive flow. But you can sometimes decline those meetings and suggest alternative times. This is harder the more people are invited to the meeting, but do what you can. If someone schedules a project update meeting or a design review meeting and it is just you and them or a small number of people, push back a little on that and suggest times that work better for you. Suggesting a time works better than just outright declining. You can't control everything to suit you, but control the things you can and take that as a win.

- **Know your meeting and calendar tools.** To do any of that stuff in the second point, you need to know how to use whatever your team uses for calendaring and you need to pay attention to the meeting invitations you get before the reminder goes off to attend. It may sound crazy obvious to say you need to know how your calendar system works, but I've helped many developers who just try to operate outside those sorts of things and *that* is not a good solution. And it isn't just the calendar. If your team uses task tracking or time tracking software, email, messaging and video conferencing systems, learn to use them effectively. You don't need to become a complete Jira expert, you don't need to reach deity-level ZOOM® usage, but all these things are part of your job and you need to be able to get around inside them and who to ask for help.

- **Organize your blocks of time.** In 2009, Paul Graham wrote an excellent piece (https://paulgraham.com/makersschedule.html) about the difference between how you as a *maker* organize your time versus how a *manager* organizes theirs. It's a quick read and it will probably have you nodding your head before you are done with it. Understanding why this difference exists won't solve the problem for you, but understanding is a good step. One thing you should take away from this understanding, though, is that you should block off chunks on your calendar for you to do your core work. Are you a morning person? Block it off. Do you do your best work right after lunch? Block it off. And you should reasonably defend it against people who schedule over it. Believe me, I've worked in teams full of smart people who seemed completely unable (or maybe just unwilling) to check whether someone was free for a meeting they wanted to schedule. If you have the time blocked, you can respond with a gentle reminder "Oh hey, saw your meeting invite, but I had to decline because that is already blocked off on my calendar. Can we do it on Tuesday afternoon instead?" You need to act like your own Executive Assistant. (By the way, notice how to do this you already need to know how to use your calendar.)

- **Limit distractions in the zone.** This final tip is a bit controversial. When you are in your times of peak productivity, limit distractions that would break flow. Close your email. Close your messaging app. Close your social media apps. You might even set an autoresponder on your email and set your status on your messaging app to indicate you are deep in work. Put your phone in a drawer. If you have an office door, close it. If you need privacy, book a small conference room and work from there or work offsite. Do whatever you can to maximize productivity when you know you are most productive.

As a (not very good) high school football player, I remember that whenever nothing else was coming out of my coach's mouth, he would just keep saying, "Fundamentals! Remember the fundamentals!"

This principle is just about the fundamentals of delivering on what we were hired to do. Not just sort of, not just so-so, but nailing it! We simply have to do that before we can do anything else.

Action Steps

- **Create a ramp up plan**
  If you are starting a job at a new company or even for a new role in the same organization, map out a 30-60-90 day plan with your manager. Write it down and talk about it in your one-on-one meetings for that onboarding period. Even if you have been in the job for awhile but you feel like you aren't getting traction, consider a 30-60-90 plan *from right now*.
- **Define your own dashboard of "good"**
  Write your own job description, just for yourself. If you look around the team and see what "average" looks like, what do you need to be doing on a regular basis to be above that? Whether you decide that is some number of bugs you need to be fixing, some number or story points you need to be delivering or whatever, come up with some clear metrics for yourself and track them.
- **Stay on top of things you're supposed to be doing**
  No matter how you track your work, that's usually the first thing you should look at every day – even if you are still in the middle of a task from yesterday. If you need to make additional to-do lists for yourself, develop that habit. If something is not going to get done, speak up. The earlier the better.

Principle #2: Make a map

When you plan to visit another country, it's helpful to learn some of the customs and practices in advance and make at least a general plan. What does "normal" look like when visiting a restaurant? Do they have Uber or taxis? What's the transit system like? What kind of places do you want to visit? Will you hire a guide or just do your own thing?

If you are visiting a place a place where another language (or even more than one) are spoken, you might want to learn at least some basic phrases in advance (after all, you need to order a sandwich, a drink or find the restroom) and you probably want some kind of dictionary or other language guide.

Principle #2 is all about establishing some basic understanding of this "work land" you are visiting.

To know how to get to a destination, you have to know where you are. You need a map. At work, there are three key elements of this map – a basic understanding of the org chart, a grasp of titles and levels, and identifying who has influence and gets things done.

Another part of building this map is understanding the culture and norms of your organization. What's "OK" and what isn't? You need to understand where the swamps and dangerous rapids are on this map so you can stay out of trouble with Human Resources and avoid misunderstandings. Finally, you need to learn the language so you can fit in like a native and navigate effectively.

The dreaded org chart

In companies where I've worked, there always seem to be those people who memorize the org chart. Spotting a change in some part of the org chart distant from their own, they might say, exasperatedly, "I see Jane Smith moved from Director of Research to VP or Operations. What do you think that means?"

I have just never been that person. It's not that one way is wrong and the other right, I just feel like I have things I need to be working on. I'm content to have a pretty strong understanding of about 2-3 levels up and a general understanding of the larger structure.

BUT get to know your org chart a little. Don't obsess over it, but know where to find it and how to navigate it. This helps you understand the overall structure of the company. If you imagine the zoomed-out org chart and you ignore the names of the people in the boxes, you can blur your eyes a bit and you begin to see how the company is structured. That's not to say it is always structured in the best way, but this is the company telling you what they think is important in the products they deliver and the way they work – because they've built that into the organization. If you see several large and deep parts of the org chart and you are off to the side in a small group, that's good to know. It may be that your small group has strong support from the Chief Technology Officer because she believes your team is working on a key future product or technology. It's not information that you are in a bad position, you could be in the best position, but it is good for you to know either way.

You don't need to obsess, just have awareness. If you know where to look when you need more details, that's the main thing.

Related to the org chart, but not always the same, is that you need to understand who are the subject matter experts (SME) or engineering "owners" of important components and systems. Particularly those that touch your work area directly. This may be a different map of its own as this kind of knowledge doesn't always fit exactly with the organization structure. If your system relies on the internal billing system, for example, it's just good to know who the one or two key people are in that team for when things go wrong.

Ladders and pay bands and titles, oh my!

Most organizations have some kind of level structure. The organization of those levels are usually organized into a "ladder," which is just a succession of levels that usually also describes the differences between, for example, a Level 1 Software Developer and a Level 2. Another term you may hear to describe this is a "Job Architecture." It is important to get an understanding of what this ladder looks like for your role family. In larger companies, this is usually pretty well documented. The trick is usually *finding* it. You should ask your manager or your Human Resources partner to direct you to it. It is usually intended to be viewable by anyone, it can just be tucked away somewhere.

The key questions you want to answer are:

- **What is my current level?** This seems an odd question, but I've seen many occasions where employees don't know their actual level or where to find that information.
- **What are the expectations for that level?** Generally, this is boiled down to a relatively short paragraph. By

itself, it is not terribly informative, but when you compare it to the description for levels below and above yours, you will see the differences.

- **How am I doing relative to those expectations?** This is really the key question, both in terms of any raises, bonuses and other rewards – such as with an annual review, as well as in terms of readiness for promotion. Don't wait until an annual review to know how you are doing. Do your own assessment and make that a topic of a discussion with your manager. Ask them for feedback on how you see yourself. This is not a conversation for every meeting with your manager, but certainly doing it quarterly would be appropriate.

- **What gaps do you need to fill in to be ready for the next level?** Look hard and introspectively at the requirements for the level you are in and the next. What do you need to do to improve your readiness for promotion? When you talk about this with your manager, be careful how you phrase it. As we'll see later, your manager can't really tell you when you will be promoted, but if you speak about it in terms of *readiness*, then that is a conversation they can have and that they should welcome.

Note that in smaller companies, this is often *not* formalized or captured in clear ways. It usually shows up around the time a company hits about 3000-5000 employees. If your organization doesn't yet have a defined job architecture, you'll want to be having conversations with your manager and your designated Human Resources team member about it.

Once you understand how the role levels are structured, you are probably wondering how they connect to pay. Levels that are associated to salary. Most often this is organized into a set of overlapping "pay bands." Other benefits and rewards may also be tied to levels – such as equity compensation, training opportunities, etc.

This is a simplified example of how pay bands are typically structured. The first chart shows how each band overlaps the one above and below it. The amount of this overlap varies, but something like 20% is relatively common. The titles and salaries are all just illustrative.

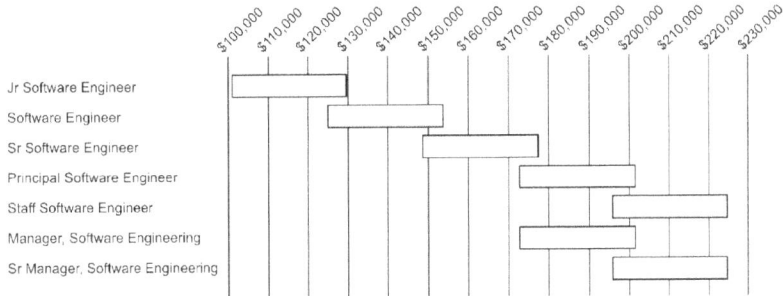

The common 20% overlap between bands aligns basically to the top and bottom "quintiles" within each band, which look like this.

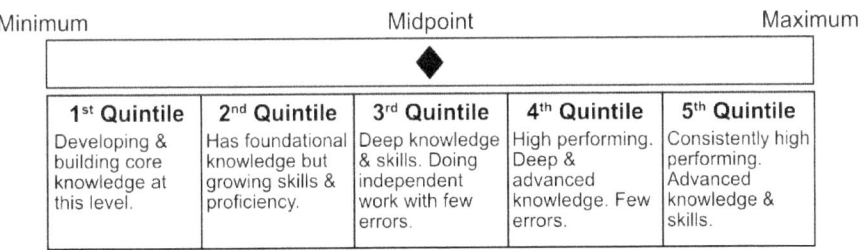

An important note about pay bands. If you have been in the same level for a while and are reaching the maximum limit of your pay band, any raises you get are going to get smaller and smaller until they stop. This is basically the system telling you that you need to get promoted to get more money.
In the diagrams above, when someone is in the 4th quintile, and certainly in the 5th, they should be being evaluated for promotion. To be a strong candidate for promotion, you

would want the person to be able to function well at the 3rd quintile of their new level. If they aren't going to be at about the midpoint in terms of skills when compared with other people in the new level, a manager might be doing them a disservice to promote them because they would struggle.

If you are wondering where you stand in the pay bands, you can ask your manager if they can tell you this. Some companies are quite open about it and others are definitely not. In still others, it really depends on the manager and what they feel about sharing the information. No harm in asking and having this additional information about how pay bands work generally will be helpful in having that discussion.

It's natural for people to think of raises as being driven by the "cost of living." If inflation is high, things cost more money so people feel like they should get raises to compensate for that. But that is **not** how it works. Compensation is based on the "cost of labor." That is, how much does it cost the company to hire someone who can do what you can do. If the economy is booming, developers are scarce and pay goes up as companies try to attract them. When the economy is slower, more engineers are available and they are, forgive me for saying, cheaper to replace. The cost of labor can be static (or even go down) even if the cost of living is high.

In *Principle #1*, we talked about using level definitions as tools you use to be great at the job you *have now*. Here, we are talking about using them as tools to progress to the *next* job in your career. In other words, not just what "good" looks like now but what the path to good looks like for your future role. The details vary quite a bit across companies, but generally what you see as you read the descriptions from the bottom level to the highest is that lower level jobs are really focused on executing work that is defined by someone higher up in that ladder. When you start out as a developer, you are usually assigned tasks by your manager. This is the "what" you need to do. Sometimes they may even be prescriptive about "how" you are to do them.

As you progress up this ladder, you are proving yourself as someone who can take on larger and larger tasks with less and less direction, and these will have a growing amount of impact on the larger product or business. You will come to the point where you are given (or even that you find for yourself) rather broadly scoped problems to solve, you communicate your progress and any needs you have from other people or teams, and everyone will assume everything is going fine unless you tell them otherwise. There comes an important career transition point from *executing* tasks to *attempting to solve* higher level problems – that may or may not have a reasonable solution. Somewhere along the way, you'll also start helping more junior team members with their tasks, which may be parts of the larger problem you are working on.

Titles are yet a different thing again. Many larger companies have established title structures that are tied with levels and are quite rigid. Other companies, and especially smaller ones, have a lot more flexibility and creativity in titles, reflecting the many hats team members often wear on small teams.

Job Title Fun

Many years ago, at Microsoft I was working on Encarta World Atlas. We had a PhD cartographer whose title in the company directory and on his business cards (remember those?) was "Spatial Data Lord."

Naturally, I was jealous of this awesome title and, not to be outdone, I immediately set out to change mine to "Multimedia Build Wizard."

Sadly, this kind of title creativity has long since passed at Microsoft and things are much more standardized.

Personally, other than for purposes of wit like that example, I've never been one to get too caught up in titles. I'm much more interested in whether I'm at the right level and how I am set up for future growth. I care more about the work I am doing and who I'm working with.

For others, and in some cultures, titles can be very important. Because the diverse way levels and titles are used in different companies and groups, it's part of your Navigation learning effort to know what they mean in your team. Just as an example, consider titles like "Product Manager," "Producer," "Program Manager" and "Project Manager." Those all sound remarkably similar, but the people in them (usually) have a definite view of what their title means. And compounding the challenge, at Company X they may mean quite different things than at Company Y, right next door. Even within the same company, titles may not be uniformly applied. All of this makes it difficult to understand the relationship between someone's title and their responsibilities.

I'll put in a plug here for talking to people. If you have team members in other job roles that you are working with and you aren't familiar with their responsibilities, sit down for coffee or lunch with them and let them tell you about their job and their goals. Most people welcome a chance to talk about themselves, so give them a chance to do that. You might ask them "what does success look like for you?" or "what is your biggest worry right now?"

Even if these things aren't things you can directly help with or control, it gives you additional context that helps you understand the larger picture. And it doesn't hurt that it also builds connections and allies that may come in handy later.

Power, influence and leadership

Who do people in your team, in your part of the organization and in your entire company pay attention to?

What names come up all the time? Whose names are mentioned in meetings or in emails from senior leaders?

In every organization, club, group or set of random people gathered in a bar, people will emerge from the crowd who are more influential. Maybe they are more convincing, maybe they are wealthier, maybe they have gained the respect of others from great work over time. However they get there, they are there. Sometimes, these are the same people who are the actual leaders of the group, but sometimes they are your peers.

This points out the difference between formal authority, or "power," that comes with a specific role – such as a club president or the CEO – and informal authority that is other people confer on a person regardless of their title. In the best of cases, there is overlap between that positional power that comes with a title and influence that basically comes from a track record that a person can be trusted to make smart and effective decisions. Make no mistake, though, they are not the same. A person can have a powerful position and not be well regarded – at least for a while, though it tends to be fleeting. And people can have strong influence over how an organization gets things done and have a modest title, possibly because they simply have different goals for their professional life.

Whether other people see you as an influencer or not at this stage, it is important to know who (or who else) is influential. People are social creatures and if you want to turbo charge your ability to get things done, you will need allies.

Note that I didn't ask whether YOU consider yourself influential. It actually doesn't matter if influencers consider themselves to be influential, although as they come to realize that, it can be helpful not just to them but to their teams as well.

Interestingly, in my research and interviews with people who are clearly influential among their fellow engineers (many of whom I also interviewed), the overwhelming majority *do not* see themselves as influential. In fact, they will outright deny it – and not just out of real or false humility. Often, they will instead talk about other people who they feel are the real influencers and thought leaders. This is true even if they are very successful in their roles and acknowledge that to be the case.

To be honest, the current definition of "influencer" with its social media implications tends to make real workplace movers-and-shakers to shy away from the word altogether.

In any case, figure out who other people listen to. This doesn't mean they are always right, by the way. It means they are thoughtful and substantive and know what they are talking about. This has given them credibility and that credibility gives them permission to have more opportunities and continue to learn and grow themselves.

How do you find them?

When you are talking with someone who you think is smart and capable, and one whom other people regard well, as part of building your relationship with them, ask *them* who they think are key influencers in the organization.

Another clue is to just listen. Whose names come up again and again?

"Let's ask _____ about this."

"This code review comment from _____ is right on target!"

You probably won't, at least immediately, build a daily coffee meetup relationship with these people. That's not the point. Just figure out who they are and watch and listen. When you see an email or some other internal communication from them, read it. Look at who they are talking to. If you have the opportunity to attend a meeting where they are speaking or presenting or proposing something, do it and just listen.

Just a note about "leadership" and the intersection it has with power and influence. Simply put, they aren't the same. Sometimes, the planets align and all three are present in one individual. Early in my career, I was fortunate enough to work in some great organizations where that has been true. As

I've gone on, though, I've had the opportunity to appreciate how genuinely rare that is.

There are lots of definitions of leadership, and this is not a book about leadership. There are many good ones on that subject. For our purposes, I think it is best expressed as a set of qualities a person has that makes other people want to follow them toward a shared goal. Someone who uses power to boss people around is not "leading." Leadership requires wise use of influence and power, but a person might have both influence and power and still not have the skills or inclination to lead. An influential person may emerge as a leader without having formal power or authority.

The discussion of all this starts to seem a little philosophical, but if you have someone in your organization who you look to as an example of what to do next and you are willing to follow them, that person is a leader. So, like art, we kind of know it when we see it.

Knowing the rules

In any group of people, even among groups of friends or family, there are things that are OK and things that are off limits. This is certainly true in companies and other organizations. There are legal limits and then somewhere separate from those purely legal limits there are other lines of what is "normal." Depending on the organization, these limits may even vary based on the team or other unit of that organization where you find yourself.

These limits may relate to what is acceptable expression in terms of language or demeanor. It might relate to conduct at team events. Or it might include how people communicate within that group of co-workers versus how they communicate externally.

I've worked on teams where bold streams of expletives flowed in team discussions, where it wasn't unusual for people to drink beer with lunch (including one company that literally had a full bar and a bartender on-site every weekday afternoon), teams where practical jokes and crude gestures were frequent, and I've worked on teams full of mild-mannered people that would never be accepting of these things. And all of these were high-functioning, productive teams of experienced professionals. Sometimes, the difference seems a matter of national culture or the industry the team operates within. Other times, it is simply the way things have ended up over time. And all of them are still subject to those legal limits on workplace behavior. Some of them have softened or evolved over time and some have not.

Here's the tricky part. Given that these rules are *unwritten*, what's the best way to learn them?

As with figuring out who the influencers are, the best way to learn these rules of conduct in the organization are to watch and listen. You are probably noticing a theme with that. It's not that there is some taboo against just asking people, "Hey what are the norms and rules of this team?" You actually could do that. You'll find in many cases, though, that the usefulness of the answers will be spotty, incomplete and sometimes even incorrect. It isn't because your team-mates want to sabotage the new guy. It's just an uncommon topic of discussion and even if they are actually following the rules themselves, it can be a hard thing to express. In fact, it may seem like common sense to them and so they won't explain in detail.

Let's compare this to software features for a moment. If you've ever watched a user study or customer focus group, you may have picked up on the fact that people, even well intentioned people, will describe how they use something in one way, but when you observe them, they actually do things *differently* then they described. It's not because they are trying to fool anyone. People are just strangely not very good at describing their own behavior or things they witness. If you are a fan of crime dramas, you have probably heard the detective characters talk about the unreliability of eyewitnesses. This falls into that same category. There are several reasons for this but a powerful (and complex) one is called "memory bias." It's a complicated topic, but a summary is that there are things that affect the way you remember things and how you categorize and rank their importance. Feel free to do some reading on the web to learn more about it. For our purposes here, it just goes back to the importance of watching how people behave in your group and listening to their conversations in meetings and around the coffee machine.

After a while, you might say something like this to a friend, "I notice that when people are gathering for standup there's lots of open conversation but then when Tom shows up, everyone kind of gets silent. What's going on there?" And then maybe the answer is "Tom has some hearing issues and a bunch of people talking at the same time is really hard for him, so we just tone it down when he shows up out of courtesy."

You've made a specific observation and that allowed you to ask a specific question that your co-worker could reasonably answer – which becomes much more useful.

As you discover the rules, you will most likely find that some of them are related to how work is done and some are purely social standards. Interestingly, the ones that affect the workflow are more likely to be written down and formally communicated, but not always.

A few general examples of group norms

- When to use Slack, when to use email or when to call a meeting.
- Special situations with team members. (like "this person has to be offline every day at 4pm sharp")
- No tolerance for workplace gossip.
- Don't cook fish in the microwave in the breakroom.
- There's no written dress code, but there is an expectation of how people normally dress for the office or for video calls.

Where does Human Resources (HR) fit?

If you have even a few months of experience, you have probably already learned this, but HR is not really there to support the employees. Their primary job is to ensure the company is safe from liability by keeping things within the bounds of the law and defined company policy.

Part of "knowing the rules" certainly includes knowing the actual legal and policy boundaries (regardless of "norms") for your own behavior as well as that of your teammates. And that means knowing when and how to involve your organization's HR team.

Because it can become complicated and isn't something you use every day (I hope!), I will cover this in the later section *When Things Go Wrong*.

Speak the language

In the tech world, we *love* our TLAs (Three Letter Acronyms) and other special tidbits of language and usage. Often, our words have different meanings than the same word used by people in other industries. If you don't believe me, ask a woodworker what a "router" is or ask a lawyer what "IP" means. Some of these terms and acronyms are industry wide and those are the easier for us to pick up and carry with us over our career. More troublesome are the dictionaries of terms that grow up within a company or part of an organization. In fact, many places I've worked have some internal resource with a list of project code names and internal acronyms. These are valuable resources to find.

Especially when you are new and still able to "play the new guy card," when you hear a term you don't know, ask someone what it means. Make a list of all the terms you learn in your notes. That new person card doesn't last forever, so learn as much as you can and then remember it and reference it so you don't have to keep asking.

As I said at the start of this principle, it is pretty difficult to get somewhere if you don't have a map and don't know where you are standing right now. Principle #2 is all about locking in those concepts. And you'll keep coming back to this exercise over and over as you move into new roles and when you change teams or companies. We all need that map at our fingertips and that's not something we grow out of.

Action Steps

- **Find your org chart.** It may be in a tool like Workday®. It could be a link on a Confluence® or another intranet page. It could even be a paper chart stuck on the wall (probably not, but you never know). Wherever it is, find it. Your manager or one of your peers who has been in the company a little longer can point you to it. Find yourself in the org chart and use it to begin to understand how your team fits into the larger organization.

- **Find a job ladder or architecture.** This is usually a table that shows the job titles and levels used in your company. Often these will be broken up by job type – like Software Developer 1, 2 and 3. Or Software Engineer, Senior Software Engineer, Staff Software Engineer, etc. Often, there will be a short explanation of what is expected of each of these levels. This will be harder to find than your org chart, but it exists somewhere. You can ask your manager. You might also ask the recruiter who you worked with when you were hired.

- **Watch, listen and take note – literally.** Pay attention to who has influence. Start cataloging norms and social rules of how things are done. Try to build a habit of capturing at least two or three brief notes each week about these things. By the way, I mentioned "memory bias." Taking notes like this is a powerful way to counteract memory bias in your own learning.

- **Find out if there's an internal acronym guide that someone has already put together and bookmark it in your browser.** This seems so basic but it really is important in ensuring you have a shared understanding of what is being discussed in the context of your current role, no matter what things were called in your last job.

Principle #3: Know your business

I can hear it now! Some of you are saying "Hey I'm a software engineer, not a Product Manager" (or vice president or sales person or *fill in the blank job title*). Absolutely true! I'm not asking you to delve into the financials, or understand all the nuances of the company strategy. No MBA is required.

What I'm talking about is to know a little about why you are doing what you are asked to do. Why does the company exist? Do you know about the core products, intellectual property and customers? How does the business work? Do customers buy the product as a one-time license or some kind of recurring subscription? Not in excruciating detail, but you should generally know the answers to those questions.

If your team uses the notion of Stories as the definition for work, an important part of a story is the "…so that…" For that individual feature or task, that's the really interesting part because it tells you what the customer for that feature is going to be able to do if you build that feature. It's the "why" of the work.

When you have that kind of view of the vision and strategy of the work you are doing, you understand how your work fits together with other work – and can spot places where perhaps it doesn't fit as well as it should. Knowing the vision and goal you are working towards allows you to use it to compare different sets of tasks or other collections of work and ask, "What gets us closer to that vision?" Or, "What does success look like?"

At its core, this is about the all-important alignment of work being done with the vision and goals of the business. Let's agree that, sometimes, that vision can be wrong. No one sets out for this to happen but people can misread markets, deliberately or not people can skew the results of analysis in a way they want, conditions can change, etc., but, for the most part, you are safer aligning yourself to that shared vision once it is defined. If you hear the vision, silently disagree with it, disregard it and just proceed on your own path – that's going to be a problem for you.

Now, if you are part of the discussion of the vision as it is being formed, which at some point in your career you will be, that is the time to speak up. Once things are solidified and a consensus formed, you have that "disagree-and-commit" moment that I talk about in *Principle #5: Don't be annoying.* How do you reach this level of alignment? Here are some useful things to incorporate in that effort:

- **Attend company and team "all-hands" meetings – and actually pay attention.** Yes, there is going to be some level of leadership drum beating and sometimes a lot of self-congratulation and that can be difficult. But there will also often be actual information about the direction of the company, changes coming down the way, new partnerships and alliances, and information about other teams and what they are doing.
- **Talk to people in your company's customer support team.** What are they hearing? What are top issues with the parts that you work on? Support teams *love it* when

engineering people listen to what they have to say and you will find out interesting things from those on the customer front-lines.

- **Talk to people in sales and marketing.** Similar to support, they are usually receptive and enthusiastic about contacts with engineering. Their perspective is going to be different yet again from Support. That is why it's great to talk to both.
- **Take advantage of "skip level" opportunities.** If your company has a culture of "skip-level one-one-ones" or "executive roundtables" which is where you have a periodic opportunity to have a one-on-one with your manager's manager or an executive, make use of that. Keep a list of questions as they occur to you and just bring one or two of these to the discussion. You'll probably have some interesting conversations and showing engagement at this level is good for you. Bare minimum, it is another touchpoint with leaders in terms of building your brand, as we'll see in *Principle #4: Manage your own brand.*
- **Use your product.** I hope this one is obvious, but you need to use whatever it is you are building. Sometimes people call this "dogfooding" (because you wouldn't buy food for your dogs from someone who didn't feed their dog food to their own dogs). It means to use your product like a customer would experience it. No secret shortcuts and backdoors. If signing up takes 10 steps for a real customer, you should go through the same process.

Even as a more junior team member, you can use an understanding of the goals and vision to help you evaluate different technical approaches to complete tasks assigned to you.
Well-known quality and management thinker W. Edwards Deming frequently shared an example about the importance

of knowing *why* we are doing a task. If you tell a team member to "clean that table" they will probably try to clean it as best as they can interpret of what you intend to use the table for. Are you cleaning the table to dismantle an engine? To serve a picnic lunch? To do surgery? Those are very different requirements. If the team member understands the purpose for which the table needs to be used, they are much more likely to clean it the way you expect. (Stocker, 2012) Flipping that around, you should proactively understand your business, your customers and your competition at least well enough to understand why you are cleaning the table.

In some teams, you may still find some of the old style feeling of "Hey, you are hired to just write the code, you don't need to know about the business." That's fading, but sadly still endures here and there.

If you face that kind of thinking, always focus your questions about the business carefully so there isn't the appearance of wanting to *change* the business goals or go into things where engineers aren't welcome, but, rather, just as someone who is trying to have "the end in mind" (as author Steven Covey wrote in the hallmark book *The 7 Habits of Highly Effective People*) so you can make sure the work you are doing on a daily basis is delivering the best value to the customer and the business.

For better or worse, we're all ultimately measured by comparing the work we do against what the business thinks is important. If we are working on a website and we optimize the sign-up flow for sheer number of new users, we'll probably build something quite different from what we would do if we were optimizing for new **paying** customers. Both could be worthwhile goals, but which one is most important to the goals of the business?

If you are a junior individual contributor, this is a conversation you should have with your team lead and your peers. If there isn't already a shared understanding on the

team, talk to your manager privately about getting that kind of information – *so that* you can make sure you are delivering the work in a way that meets those goals.
If you are the manager, and you don't have a clear picture of the business goals, talk to your manager, or the product owner or product manager for your team. Again, stress that the value isn't to argue over the goals, but to help your team deliver against them effectively.

You'll find your work is so much more effective when you understand how your pieces fit in with the larger puzzles of the business you are in. Know why you are cleaning that table.

Action Steps

- **Know *your* customer.** For your job, not your company or your product, answer the question, "who is my customer?" Who expects you to deliver things to them and what are those things? This may be someone external that we conventionally think of as a "customer" or it may be another internal team who depends on your work.
- **Know the vision.** For whatever you are currently working on – a coming release, a live service, or an internal project – what is the vision for that project? Usually, this is boiled down to just a few sentences and captured in a document somewhere.
- **Understand the business basics.** Learn three basic things about your company and the business it is in:
  - Who are your customers?
  - What problem are you solving for those customers?
  - How do customers pay for whatever you are providing? Subscription? Fee for services? A one-time purchase?
- **Find the metrics.** Find out if there is there any kind of internal dashboard where you can see how your team, division or company is doing against its goals?

Principle #4: Manage your own brand

Everyone is known to their co-workers, friends and family as something.

I'm not a super-fan of the chatter around a "personal brand." It just feels a little too "influencer" to the Gen X in me, and I see that as someone trying to get me to buy running shoes or skin care products. The truth is, though, that we each have a "brand" whether we want to or not. Whether you call it "reputation," "image," "persona" or "brand," it is something that surely exists in the minds of people who know us or work with us. It is worth spending just a little effort on it to make sure it is the image or reputation that *you* want to be conveying about your main product – yourself. Boiled down to its essence, the principle of managing your work (and maybe into your non-work life) brand is to ensure you are known for something *valuable*. It's fine to be viewed as someone with a sense of humor, or someone who cares about others, but if you aren't *also* seen as doing something valuable for the team or the organization, those other traits won't help your career.

In my decades of working in software engineering, and my many hours of interviewing software professionals for this book, I have learned that one of the most difficult things for developers to do in terms of managing their brand and their career is to grasp the importance of **visibility**. Maybe it goes against what, for many of us are our, perhaps, slightly introverted tendencies. It feels like political games, and most of us view "office politics" as a very negative thing. The fact is, much as I said about "influence" in *Power, influence and leadership* under *Principle #2: Make a map*, anytime there is a group of people doing anything, there is politics. Politics is just how people relate to each other within a structure. True, taken to the extreme, workplace politics leads to a toxic, stagnant, or just unpleasant situation. I'm not advocating climbing up the corporate ladder by knocking down your co-workers.

As an example, one of the aspects of my brand that I actively try to cultivate is that I want to be seen as, and to actually be, someone who tries to lift up other people so that the whole team gets better over time. This means that, yes, sometimes I skip lunch to help someone find out where they can look for information themselves or explain to them how to use the org chart to find the people they need to ask for some information they need to complete their task. And, yes, sometimes this means I work later hours to do my own tasks because I did that. I don't do this because I want people to think I'm awesome, I just think it is the right thing to do, but it *does* reflect on me professional as well.

You may be wondering how you do this without looking like an attention-grabbing monster. The key is a sense of moderation. Right now, I can almost promise you that you are doing *too little* in this area, so there is some safe distance to go before you risk over-doing it. Let's work through some practical steps.

Your goal

As I've counseled and advised people many times over the years, if you want to nurture your career, a key aspect is that people outside of your immediate work team need to know your name.

Just let that sink in for a minute.

By "know your name," I mean two things. One, they need to know you exist on the team; *literally* they need to know your name. Two, they need to know something good about you – that you know a ton about Git or that you are fluent in Spanish, which happens to be important for one of your project partners right now. Just something.

One of the things that typically separates each level of engineers (or any role, really) in a "career ladder" description is the "breadth of impact" – which is just another way of saying "who knows your name?"

This means a level 3 developer is expected to have a contribution that in some way touches more parts of the product or company than a level 2 engineer. A level 5 dev will have even more of an impact than the level 3.

You can visualize this as ripples in a pond, where the circles are going out different distances and meeting up with others who are making their own impacts. When done in a healthy way, these different efforts aren't conflicting with one another or jockeying for domination, or putting other people down. Rather they are additive. That's the goal and what "good" looks like.

There is a bare minimum level of impact to have any level of sustainable success in a role. If you are an individual contributor developer, of course that starts with your immediate team. Whether you call it a "Feature Team," a "Scrum Team" or a "Pod," those co-workers and leads need to know who you are and recognize your contributions. The next step up in that minimum tier is your project or product team. This may be many dozens of people. They also need to know what you are bringing to the table in terms of delivering value to the team and the customer.

Beyond that, you step upward through Departments and Divisions or Business Units. Different organizations will have different terminology, but you can see from the diagram below how that impact and influence expands. It becomes difficult to be promoted to Principle and Staff level roles without the support of directors, vice presidents and engineers already in those roles. Those people have to know you when it comes time to evaluate who will get those promotions.

And expanding even further, to the highest levels of your company – perhaps you want to position yourself to be doing technical demonstrations on stage at big events or with key customers. Even if something like that is well outside your normal comfort zone.

Further still, we get into the more rarified air of people who become known in their industry and even across industries. People who speak up in setting standards and defining the ways people work.

Along the way, the level of difficulty in having an impact does go up significantly, and the number of people operating at each level become fewer.

Dennis Ritchie was a software engineer at Bell Labs when he helped create the Unix operating system and the C programming language.

Anders Hejlsberg was a software engineer working on a Pascal compiler that became Borland's Turbo Pascal and then the chief architect for the Delphi language and ultimately the lead architect for C# and TypeScript at Microsoft.

Clearly it is possible to rise to this level if that is your goal and where you want to devote your energies.

The level of impact goes with your career level. No one expects a junior dev to have the same impact as a staff engineer with perhaps decades of experience.

Even as a junior engineer, it's obvious that your immediate team-mates need to know you, and that your manager knows you. That is just basic table stakes.

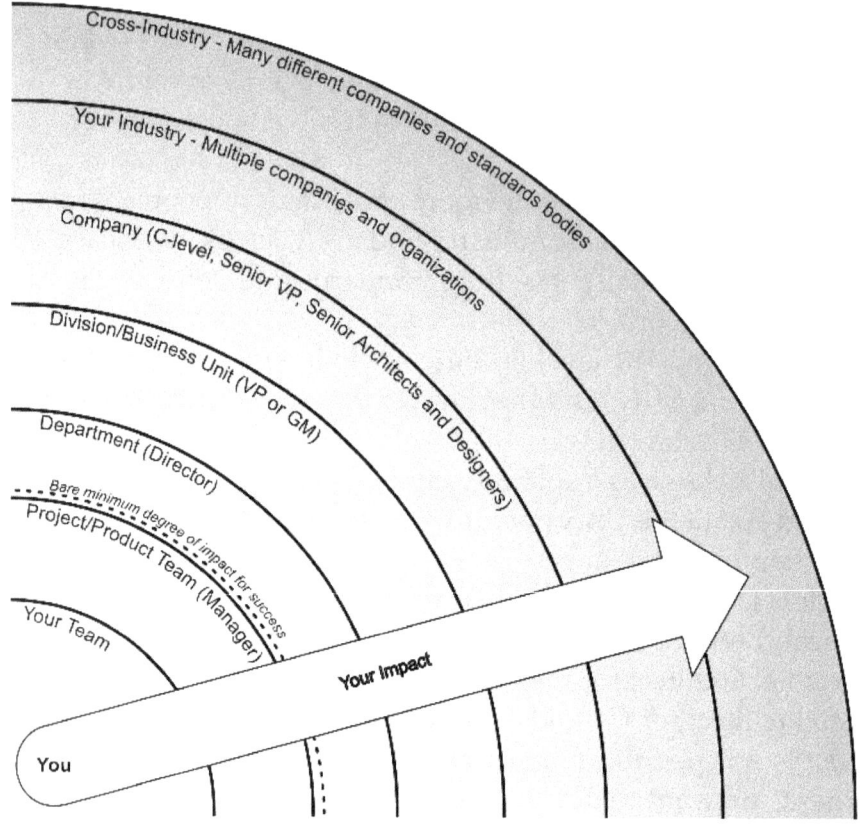

Now you need to find ways for other engineers in the larger team, and their managers, to get to know you, as shown by the grey highlighted parts of this simplified example. Later in the book, in *Beyond the essentials*, I'll talk about "brown bag" or "lunch and learn" sessions. This is an excellent low-friction way that is ideal for engineers to get to know who you are and for you to build your brand. Also, never underestimate the power of watching and listening. Don't be too eager to jump in and comment on every discussion. In some ways, that might make it seem like you don't have much to occupy your time, even if that isn't true.

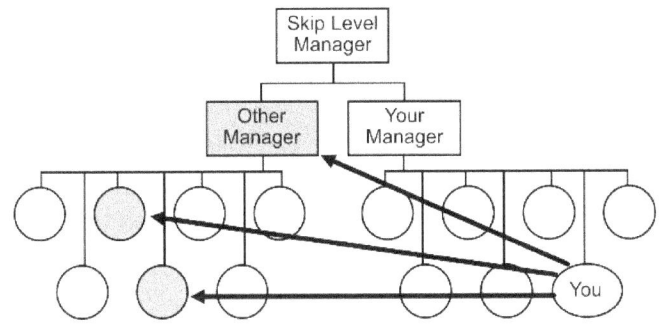

Building and strengthening your network

In *Principle #2: Make a map*, we touched tangentially on this idea of building up your network but let's dive in a little deeper on that.

When we hear about "building our network," we might have an image of a *quid quo pro* or some kind of nepotism. Basically, building a network of people we will *use* in some way to further our own purposes. I think as most of us are on LinkedIn and have an understanding of our "social graphs," maybe this feeling is less prevalent now.

If you really are a person who only has friends so you can take advantage of them, I guess my advice to you would be "stop doing that." People don't like it, it is more obvious than you think, and it violates *Principle #5: Don't be annoying*. It tends to catch up to people and you'll find yourself on the outside of what you thought was your network.

This is about building a network of people who you can learn from, serve, consult and exchange ideas with. This is different from the way most people see their social media followers, friends or connections in that these are people you actually know and have some level of personal and professional trust. It's a two-way relationship where you are able to help each other.

Real relationships are based on trust. This doesn't have to be some elaborate commitment or subscribing to a shared manifesto of some kind. In *Principle #1: Nail your job,* you read about doing what you say you will do. That's how you build trust. It's really no more complicated than that. If someone asks you to take a look at some code you are working on and you tell them you can do it by noon tomorrow, then you need to either do it by noon tomorrow, or, if something has come up to change that, you need to get back to them. When you keep your commitments like that, you are showing people respect and that is central to building that relationship of trust. Look for opportunities to add value by serving people you want to bring into your network. It's not all strictly business either. Look for chances to socialize at team or company events, grab lunch or coffee, or even just ask how they are doing and listen to their answer. Showing real empathy to your co-workers is a always great thing to cultivate.

If your company has a feedback system, where you can request anonymous feedback from other employees, asking for feedback is also a great way to strengthen relationships in your network. When you ask someone for feedback, even if they don't end up providing any because they feel like they are too busy or whatever, that registers as you showing you trust them. They'll remember that, and perhaps you'll see feedback requests about them. (We'll cover giving effective feedback later in the book.) In general, if you look for

> **empathy** noun
> em-pa-thy
> The action of understanding, being aware of, being sensitive to, and vicariously experiencing the feelings, thoughts, and experience of another.
> "empathy," Merriam-Webster.com Dictionary

opportunities for other people to achieve their goals and to build them up, they will reciprocate. Just be prepared that this is not *always* true. There are definitely people who would take advantage of you. This is not advice that you should just weakly accept that kind of treatment. Don't feel like you need to maintain relationships with people who attempt to take advantage of you beyond the bare minimum required for you to do your job.

Become an expert and an owner

Make yourself essential. Yes, I know, easy to say, but the fact is, relative to your teammates, you probably either already are, or are close to being, an expert on some tool, business or technology partner, component or some unique piece of intellectual property the team is responsible for.

Related to being an "expert" on something, you can also become the "owner" of something. These two things are somewhat related, but they don't have to be directly the same. You can become the owner of something, especially if it is something that other people *don't want to own* (see "eating the frog" in the *Sign up for extra* section). In fact, becoming the owner of something can be a great step to becoming an expert.

Take a personal brand inventory

When I'm interviewing candidate for a position on my team, I have already read their resume and I have it right in front of me, but I'll usually ask them, "Tell me what kind of person you are." This is kind of backdoor way of asking them to tell me about their brand.

Are they primarily a frontend dev who has full stack skills but would always rather do frontend? Is she really a cloud database person who struggles with web frameworks but can write basic code to test her own database changes?

There's no wrong answer and it's not a "do or die" situation. I just want to hear them summarize all that they have done and want to do in just few sentences.

As you contemplate how you will manage your brand, I'd challenge you to invest some time thinking about yourself. What kind of person do YOU think you are? How do you want other people to perceive you? What's the difference between who you are right now and who you want to be? It's completely OK to be aspirational, so long as *you* know whether you are talking about a trait you have or one you want to develop. In a sense, we're talking about both who you *are* and who you *want to become*.

Make a spreadsheet, a document or a page in your paper notebook with two columns and label them "Now" and "Desired." Start to fill the rows of these columns with traits and characteristics. The list of possibilities is basically endless, but here are a few to start your thinking.

- Takes on hard things
- Curious
- Knowledgeable of, or expert in _____ some specific technology C#, Internet of Things (IoT), cloud computing, machine learning - whatever
- Helps others
- Sees the big picture
- Data-driven
- Customer focused
- Open-minded
- Pragmatic
- Estimates accurately
- Quality obsessed
- Self-aware

You should also talk to close friends outside of work, someone with whom you are in a relationship, or other people who can help you assess yourself through different eyes.

If you need help thinking broadly about your strengths, you can find a variety of resources with a web search, and there's always Don Clifton's classic *StrengthsFinder* books and assessments which some people find helpful.

You may find it helpful to review this process and your list with your manager or your mentor. This can become a great lattice-work for effective career development discussions.

Once you have a version (because you'll continue to iterate on it over time) of your brand inventory, you should actually use it. For example, before you go into a design review meeting, look over the current strengths on your list. How can you work these into your meeting preparation? For example, if you want to be seen as a data-driven person, you should focus your questions and discussion in a data-driven way. This reinforces that trait as part of your brand.

Raising your visibility – without "grandstanding"

How do you improve your visibility and make more of an impact in ways that feel real and genuine?

Start by just speaking up

Start by simply speaking up. Most of us have regular opportunities – daily stand ups, planning and retrospective meetings, one-on-one meetings with our managers, and so on. If you watch the dynamic on most teams, you usually see the same handful of people offering opinions or participating actively. You've probably felt like you had something to say and maybe held yourself back. Look for opportunities to just engage in the conversation. Remember, you aren't looking to dominate the conversation, just to participate in a thoughtful way.

Maybe you have a different opinion on the importance of a bug, maybe you think someone may be forgetting something when they offer an estimate for a task. Set a goal to become a more active presence on the team. Of course, participating in meetings means you need to be a focused listener and pay attention to what is going on, which is also a good thing. This is how you will find out about the struggles and ideas other team members are having and perhaps you will be the person to help or build on those.

Even in routine tasks like code reviews you can leave a comment or two, even if they are positive things, before you click that approve or accept button.

Another way to start speaking up is by asking questions.

There's an unfortunately common belief that asking questions makes you look unintelligent or, even worse, argumentative. Asking questions is how we all move from ignorance to informed on any topic. Even if our question is answered with numerous conflicting opinions from different people, that in itself is information. Yes, questions can be used in an aggressive way to drive division and contention. But what I'm talking about is honest questions to fill in gaps in understanding. For example: "Why are we prioritizing these user interface changes when we know design is working on a full revamp of the UI soon? Won't that just be wasted effort?" This is a question about the prioritization of two different sets of work and totally reasonable.

> "If I had an hour to solve a problem and my life depended on the solution, I would spend the first 55 minutes determining the proper question to ask...for once I know the proper question, I could solve the problem in less than five minutes."
>
> Albert Einstein

One place that can cause difficulty is if the same person asks the same question repeatedly over time. This is especially true with "How do I..." kinds of process questions. This is a problem because it indicates the person asking the question for the N-th time is not learning and doesn't respect other people's time enough to even write down the answer they got last time.

All of this discussion about speaking up applies equally to both face-to-face meetings as well as email, messaging threads, code and document reviews, wiki discussions and any other form of communication. Be an active, vocal member of the team – but not so much so that other people on the team come to believe you must not have anything else to do except comment on things. Most people won't go that far, but you could even decide that you are going to limit yourself to some small number of comments and interjections per day.

Look for things to improve – and improve them

As we go through our normal day, all of us run into things that cost us time. Missing or incorrect documentation, clumsy workflow steps that require manual interventions, or just annoying things that are in our face every day. The next time you see one of those that is truly small and contained, take it on yourself to fix it. This might require you to learn some new things along the way to do it. You don't even have to tell anyone you are doing it until it is ready for other people to try. Just grab something and get it done. People will really appreciate it because if it annoys you it annoys them too.

If the task is larger or touches other parts of the code or process, then advocate that it be planned into a coming sprint or other increment of work and volunteer to take it on.

This also applies to the way you personally do things. You should always be finding and using good habits. How do you do that? Well, where do we get any of our professional (and even personal) habits? We might learn them from formal education in school, but just a note that especially for software engineers, most university programs don't teach very good practices and habits, though there are exceptions. We might learn them from things we read, but really, we spend most of our lives observing and learning them from other people, especially those whom we particularly respect. Once you develop good habits personally, you can begin to turn those habits into effective systems for ourselves and for our teams. Something like the coding standards you've probably seen in your company are just good habits that have been written down, argued over and agreed and turned into a system. You could consider Test Driven Development (TDD) as another example of something that just started as a good, healthy habit that has grown into a widely-used practice.

You may not be the next Ken Schwaber (or, maybe you will), but all of us are fully capable of finding things that work better than what we may be doing now, applying it in our own work and convincing others that it is helpful. And this is a powerful way to build your visibility and impact and grow your personal brand.

Share what you are doing

Make sure your manager is aware of your achievements, and regularly, not just when you are compiling an annual or quarterly review.

If someone on your team other than your manager is responsible for assembling a periodic status report or other message that communicates progress to the broader team, make sure they are aware of notable work you've done. Not every bit of good work gets covered in messages like this, but your goal is just to make sure what you are doing is known to the people who can share it. In the section *Be a sharer, not a hoarder* I will introduce the subject of "weeklogs" which can become another tool for you to share with the team and beyond.

Sign up for extra

Another way to raise your profile as an engaged and valuable contributor is to --- volunteer for assignments and tasks that just need to be done. I know, the idea of signing up for some set of additional work when you may already feel you have a lot on your plate doesn't seem like a great idea. In my own career, I've personally made a point to do this, sometimes even with things that require significant sacrifice for a period of time. Taking on hard tasks and doing them well, has been a key part of *my* brand.

The important part of this is that not only do you need to be willing to accept these additional jobs, but you do have to actually deliver on them. If you sign up for extra things and then don't do them or do them poorly, that will *not* help you. People will still take notice, but not in a good way.

These extra tasks don't all have to be impossibly difficult. Sometimes they are just time consumers – interviewing a lot of candidates, mentoring an intern, being an on-boarding buddy for a new hire, or signing up for a recruiting trip to your *alma mater* are not horrible things, in fact sometimes they are actually fun, but they do take us away from our planned tasks and so people tend not to raise their hand when they come up. Find things that work for you and do them. As an example, many years ago I was a guest lecturer in a programming class at a community college for several days, which was not really any work for me and we had some very great discussions. More recently, I gave a short presentation about mobile game development at a kids' coding camp and gave the kids feedback on their game jam projects. Full disclosure, I also did a project that involved a very challenging partner and very heavy travel over an 18-month period. That was very difficult for my home life, but it was a sacrifice we chose to make for that time.

This practice of taking on a hard thing and just getting it done is sometimes called "eating the frog." Once you have eaten that frog and the hard, unpleasant thing is out of the way, other things won't seem so bad – and you'll be remembered as "that guy who ate the frog." In a January 2024 article on *Business Insider*, Andrew Yeung elaborated on his experience growing his career by eating a lot of frogs. He suggests looking for things your manager is spending a lot of time doing and doesn't like to do, learning how to do them and doing them well. This is great perspective on the real-world application of this technique.

> The phrase "eat the frog" comes from the 18th century French writer Nicolas Chamfort who reportedly said, "A man should swallow a toad every morning to be sure of not meeting with anything more revolting in the day ahead."
> (This is often attributed to Mark Twain, but it appears Mssr. Chamfort is the true source.)

Imposter Syndrome, the great saboteur

As you work to build your brand, an old nemesis may raise its head. If you are like me, you probably felt imposter syndrome long before you knew it had a name. This is the feeling that causes you to doubt your skills, credentials, experience and abilities and to think you are not as good as your peers and are on the verge of being discovered as a fraud and a failure. It can make us feel guilty when we succeed, because we feel like we "slipped through" and haven't really earned it. Even if *intellectually* you know this is not true, *emotionally* it can still cause fear and discomfort, and in extremes can lead you to sabotage your own career progress or keep you from taking chances or working toward promotions or positions of greater responsibility.

There is a well-known quote from Steve Jobs, "Everything around you that you call life was made up by people that were no smarter than you and you can change it, you can influence it, you can build your own things that other people can use."

You've probably heard this before, and maybe felt like for some reason he was only talking to "smarter people."

In the introduction, I mentioned my "terror" when our small company was acquired by Microsoft in 1994. How could I ever fit in there? Weren't they all smarter than me? I discovered that while, yes, there were a lot of smart people there, I did, in fact, fit in and was able to contribute and innovate. Working with other smart people makes you smarter. Yet, decades later, when I was hired at Amazon, the same worries bubbled up again. Again, I found that I fit in just fine.

It's hard to imagine why our minds are wired this way. It's not even recognized as a mental disorder; it's just how people are. Recognizing that this is true, we can be in a better position to push back on these feelings we sense them coming on.

> **The ultimate example of self-confidence**
> It may seem a strange connection to make, but consider this story of the capture of Vienna's Tabor Bridge during the Napoleonic wars.
> In 1805, the Austrian and Russian armies were in retreat and Vienna was abandoned. The French Grande Armée moved

into the city, but the important bridges across the Danube were guarded by Austrian artillery and rigged with explosives. Thinking fast, Napoleon's Marshals Lannes and Murat, along General Bertrand and quite a few of their staff officers, calmly approached the bridge, unarmed. They called out and waved in a very friendly way. When challenged by an Austrian sentry they excitedly shared the news that a treaty had been signed and the Austrians were now allied with the French. Amazingly, they managed to sell this to the soldiers protecting the bridge, and to Count Auersperg who commanded the defenders.

A suspicious Austrian sergeant actually lit the fuse that would have demolished the bridge, but Lannes snuffed it out – and then berated the sergeant for attempting to damage public property and threatening to have him punished.

The French officers chatted with the defending troops excitedly about the new treaty and their friendship – while a large column of French Grenadiers crossed the bridge and disarmed all of the Austrians – which is when they knew they'd been fooled.

The next time you feel a bout of imposter syndrome coming over you, think of this story. If these guys could pull this off, you can certainly show a demo of your new feature at a division meeting or make your case for why React would be better than Angular for the next generation web app the team is building.

You probably noticed this principle is different from the first three. This is the place where you decide how you want people to see you. What you want to be known for, and creating a marketing plan for yourself. From my years of leading and coaching other engineers, I *know* that the biggest stumbling block we have as a group is figuring out how to appropriately draw attention to our own work. We're sometimes so afraid of either being noticed at all or of going too far the other direction and making a scene. More than any other topic in this book, *this* is the thing you have to figure out to get to the places you want to go in your career.

Action Steps
- **Do an initial personal brand inventory.** This section gives you some starting ideas. Create a recurring time slot on your calendar to revisit your inventory periodically. After the initial effort, it would be good to come back to it weekly for a few weeks, and then switch to a longer period, monthly or quarterly. If you already have time set aside to review your goals, this would be a natural thing to add to that.
- **Share your brand inventory.** In your next one-on-one with your manager, share the brand inventory you've created. Discuss it and ask for feedback. Talk about how the areas you identified can best align with the work the team is doing.
- **Cultivate your interests.** Foster your areas of interest by finding other people inside or outside of your company who have similar areas of focus. There may be Slack channels in your company for technologies or best practices that are on your list (or you could create them), outside meetups, even like-minded people who get together for lunch now and then.
- **Find ways to contribute.** Look for high-profile projects inside the company to which you can contribute. Depending on your available time and company policy, you might also look at open source public projects or personal projects. *Make sure you understand any rules that apply to outside projects before you start.*

Principle #5: Don't be annoying

Should this really be a principle? You'd like to think not, but we are all humans and if you are reading this book you are generally a pretty driven kind of human and maybe one who doesn't have a lot of patience with others of our same type of human. Some clashes are inevitable. We have different opinions of how best to do things – even if all those opinions might be equally good or nearly so. We have different experiences we bring to work. And let's not forget that we are often operating under significant pressure.

What does it mean to "be annoying"?

Pointing out a mistake - poorly. For example, someone may have implemented something that seems to operate correctly but will have other implications in terms of performance, scale, compatibility, standards or whatever. In short, they didn't do a great job with it. If you point that out, even during a review session, that person will probably find it annoying. In this example, pointing out the mistake is the right thing to do. The only mitigation against someone taking it as annoying is *how* you communicate that. Keep it professional and based on facts. If you have data or examples of how this has impacted the team when other people have done it, so much the better. And if you can come up with an example where *you* made a similar mistake yourself, that's better still. Keep this kind of feedback about the *thing* not the *person*. Anything sounding like "Bob you *always* forget about this!" is **not** the right way.

Allowing people to feel like you don't respect them. You might ask yourself why I didn't simply say "disrespecting people." It's an important difference. Most of us (unless we are *truly* annoying) don't go around intentionally disrespecting people – and that's good. More important than how we think we are treating people is how another person *perceives* we are treating them. Yes, maybe this begins to sound a little "soft" for us engineer types, but it is important. We need to go an extra step to try to ensure the other person doesn't feel we are talking down to them, that we are interrupting them, or belittling their expertise. It can be difficult, even if we are trying to do the right thing and we can never control what another person thinks, all we can do is try a little harder to make them feel comfortable in that discussion. There can be a strong cultural element to this – and by that, I mean both the actual demographic cultures of the people involved in the exchange, as well as the organizational or team culture. And, I'm just going to say this, while it has improved, I still see a lot of male engineers using big voices to talk over female engineers in meetings. Or coders speaking condescendingly to non-developer roles – like design or product management. The short version of all of that is *don't treat people like you think they aren't smart*. Turns out people really don't like that.

Wasting people's time. This is actually a form of disrespecting people but it is important enough to stand on its own. In our work lives, time is often our most precious commodity. Time is how we measure work progress and if people see you as wasting their time, you are really standing directly in the way of them getting things done they see as important. The number one way we waste other people's time is to interrupt them when they are in their "flow" state. Software development is very much based on flow (also known as being in "the zone"). When a developer is deep in the zone and you come by their desk and ask them a question, it can take them 20 minutes or more for them to get their mind back to where it was. And if the interruption was, for example, to ask a question that you should have been able to figure out yourself but you thought it was just faster (for you) to ask someone rather than look, they **are** going to resent that. One-hour meetings that could have been 20 minutes, meetings that could have been emails, emails that could have been Slack messages, and spamming the team channel with pictures of your cat are all on that time-waster spectrum.

Always trying to re-open a closed decision. When the team has a decision in hand, if you want to revisit that decision, particularly if you are seen as someone who keeps trying to revisit that same decision, it is really going to annoy people. Decisions are precious. They let the team move forward and start putting solutions in place. Refighting those battles is seen as blocking all of that progress and feels like chaos. When a decision has been made, you have three choices.

1) Embrace it and move on.
2) Disagree and commit. I'm stealing an old Amazon Leadership Principle there. Basically, state your disagreement as part of the decision-making process, but then you either need to commit yourself to the chosen path, or if you absolutely can't do that, you probably need to find a different job, or at least a different team in the company.
3) Revisit because of new data. If you actually have data that impacts a previously closed decision, then you should raise that. As part of that you should state clearly what the data show, why it wasn't part of the original discussion, and how it impacts the decision.

If you do something other than those three things, people aren't going to be very happy with that. And if you develop a reputation as someone who does this repeatedly, it's going to become an obstacle for you professionally.

Being a *prima donna*. No one wants to work with people who are just overtly offensive and difficult. People who seem to go out of their way to make waves don't get invited to parties. Similarly, though, when someone is difficult to work with because they take every comment or bit of feedback as a personal attack or insult, even if they have to apply the most twisted reading to the situation to make that true, other work mates are going to find that annoying. No matter how good you are at your job, if your co-workers feel like they have to walk on eggshells around you, they aren't going to like that. The modern workplace can be a difficult minefield. If someone is seen as one who takes offense constantly, people will not want to expose themselves to what they may see as a career risk. Some might say we need "thick skins" or a workplace persona that is "tough." I don't necessarily agree with that. I do think we should "Assume Positive Intent." Just remember the programmer friendly acronym "API." Our first step when someone says something should be to assume they aren't trying to hurt our feelings personally. And having done that, we can try to figure out what they *were* trying to say. This is especially important with asynchronous communication like Slack and e-mail. It might sound crazy at this point in history, but these are the times it just pays off to pick up the phone and make a voice call, or stop by the other person's desk in person.

Being a glory hound. This might seem counter to what I said in *Principle #4* about making your work visible. There is a balance here that you will need to find. Three hard and basic rules to help you get started.

1) Don't take credit for work other people did – even if the person who did the work is no longer with the team and even if that person isn't speaking up for

themselves. People will eventually (and pretty quickly) see through this and just stop paying attention to what you say. It costs you credibility and that is incredibly hard to come back from.

2) Don't take credit for things that didn't actually happen. This may sound ridiculous, but if you pay attention, this happens all the time and very little will get you tuned out faster than this. Don't take credit for things you *plan* to do. Don't take credit for things *you are proposing* to do. Save it for when you have a meaningful, demonstrable achievement. Remember, "done" is a binary state. Don't brag about things being "80% done" or "all done except testing."

3) Don't turn team accomplishments into your personal accomplishments. It's fine if you are the one broadcasting the story, but be generous in mentioning people by name who genuinely took part in the work and say what they did.

Being argumentative. Engineering disciplines as a whole tend to involve some degree of argument. We're all searching for the "best" way. Unfortunately, we don't all share the same notion of "best" nor a shared vision of how to get there, so we sometimes try to argue our way to agreement. There's an acceptable level of that. It becomes annoying if you have a reputation of just being difficult and argumentative, always taking the "devil's advocate" position and arguing things you may not even strongly believe, and being seen as unpredictable and explosive as an old stick of dynamite. People will just start excluding you if that becomes true. When you are going to engage in a disagreement, make sure you, first and foremost, really care enough to have that disagreement. Is it a big enough deal for you or for the product? Is it something that, even if you feel the other person is wrong, they can just own it and try it and find out for themselves? Sometimes there is real learning value in just letting people do it their way; not everything is worth a battle.

Make sure if you are disagreeing you keep that disagreement appropriate to your workplace culture in tone and language and make sure you are arguing about the thing, not the person. Which brings us to our last annoyance…

Making it personal. If you find yourself in a discussion and hear yourself saying, or hopefully catch yourself *about* to say, things like "you always…," "you've never understood…," "you just haven't had enough experience to see…" or basically anything that involves the word "you," **STOP**. If you've already said it, apologize on the spot in front of whomever heard it. *Ad hominem* attacks can severely impact your reputation and limit your growth probably faster than anything – and quite possibly find you and your manager in a discussion with Human Resources. Just don't. Once people see you as this kind of person, it is very difficult to recover.

The opening sentence of this section asks if this should even need to be a principle. Originally, there were just the first four. At some point in my interviews with engineers, the experiences they shared convinced me this was enough of a problem that it deserved top billing with the others and was promoted from a few paragraphs somewhere else to principle status. If you nail your job and understand your organization and business and market your brand carefully, but you are still a painful person to work with and someone who leaves wreckage in your wake on every project, you will not reach your potential. Yes, there was a time early in my career where people made their point by punching their fist through a conference room wall or throwing chairs. I lived that (and did some of it). That ***does not work anymore***, thank goodness! As with the old kindergarten report cards, we are graded on whether we work and play well with others.

Action Steps

- **Practice "active listening."** Even if you are genuinely engaged and listening in a conversation, reflecting back what someone has said does two important things. First, it lets them know you heard them, even if you don't agree fully and, second, it provides a way to immediately clear up the difference in what you think you heard and what they think they said. Just try it. "So you are saying we should change the code review process we've been using to require a minimum of two reviewers for any substantial change? How would you define 'substantial'?"

- **Get control of runaway digital discussions.** If you are part of a discussion that is bouncing back and forth in email or messaging for more than a couple rounds, get the participants together. That can mean standing at a whiteboard together, in a meeting, on a video or phone meeting. You'll be surprised how much faster this gets to a useful conclusion. Then summarize the outcome in that email or messaging thread. Or, write a short document that captures the current state of the discussion and circulate it with the participants. Look for opportunities to do this when discussions are just circling.

- **Be introspective.** Do a thoughtful personal inventory about the things we covered in this principle. We all have some of these habits in our nature. Think about feedback you've had from managers and peers, and even in your personal life. Pick out one or two things – **just one or two** – and work on improving. If you work from home, put a sticky note on the edge of your monitor to remind you, or inside your laptop, someplace you will see it when you are likely to do whatever that annoying thing is.

Beyond the essentials

The five principles cover the basics, but now what? Once you have a grasp of those core concepts, what other tools do you need?

The good news (for you) is that if you look around at your peers, you will probably see that most of them aren't aware of the challenges they face in their career, or if they are, the solutions seem mysterious, arbitrary and elusive. Just by starting to ask questions and seek guidance, you will already be better equipped, even with the basics we've already covered.

This section is a collection of additional information, tactics and techniques that will help you build your career success. Some of these, like the discussion about the impact of artificial intelligence on our jobs and the section about things your manager will never tell you, came up repeatedly in interviews. This made them seem worth covering, even though they don't necessarily "fit" so cleanly.

Be a communicator

Even as a junior developer, your ability to communicate both in writing and verbally is very important. Most engineers, certainly before they get to the principal and staff level, aren't spending large parts of their day in meetings and aren't presenting to rooms full executives, customers or partners, but you need to be able to ask questions and answer questions from others in a coherent and succinct way.

You may have worked with someone (or perhaps you are like this) that answers the exact question that is asked and only that question – like the Oracle of Delphi in the example below. Often, if you think for a moment about the context of the question, you might want to ask some clarifying questions to make sure you are giving the most useful answer.

Ask clarifying questions
Greek legends tell us of a priestess at the Temple of Apollo known as the Oracle of Delphi. She would answer questions, but it mattered a great deal how the question was phrased. There is a story that in 560 BC, King Croesus of Lydia consulted the Oracle as to whether he should make war on the Persians. The Oracle responded that if he attacked the Persians he would "destroy a mighty empire."

*Taking this as a good sign, he attacked, and lost. **His** empire was destroyed rather than that of the Persians.*

In hindsight, King Croesus probably should have asked a follow up question or two.

I observed a discussion once where a director asked an operations person, "How much are we spending on cloud compute for product x?" The ops engineer looked it up and gave a dollar figure.

The director said, "Wait a second. I'm looking at a finance report and they are saying it is nearly double that."

Ops engineer looks again and says, "Oh, do you mean the dev and test environments too. That's this amount..."

In this example, the ops engineer assumed the director meant for production only and just gave that number. Not

> completely unreasonable, but he could have easily either
> answered with the cost breakdown for the three
> environments or asked if she meant only production.

The confusion in this example was simple enough to resolve in this face-to-face discussion, but imagine if it were email or messaging. Imagine if the director had not questioned that number and used it to respond to a question from the VP. It's worth clarifying an ambiguous question ahead of time. This level of engaged thinking is how you can deliver clear value.

Beyond questions and answers, your communication is really *the way* that you present yourself to others. What you say in a daily stand-up, interviewing a candidate, responding to points someone raises when reviewing your code for a check-in, talking through your design on a whiteboard, even your body language; it's all communication.

Communication always takes up a certain slice of your time, even in less senior engineering roles. As you progress from less to more senior positions, that "communication" slice of the day will expand. A staff engineer spends most of their time and effort in communications of various sorts and a small slice, maybe 25%, writing code with their own hands.

An often-ignored aspect of effective communication is understanding that different people respond to different forms of communication. There's not a science or a formula to this – like "ah this is a very busy person so they will like email." Particularly for the most important relationships – your manager, your product owner, etc. – you really should just ask them. Since it is valuable to *you* that your communication be effective this is an example where you it's just best to adjust to the styles of the consumers of your message.

If you are communicating something in email or messaging that is genuinely and necessarily long or detailed, include a summary right at the top of your email. This "tl;dr" should be enough to hit the key points and if you need an answer or specific action, include that at the top as well. Don't make people dig for the thing you want them to do. This is sometimes referred to as the "Bottom Line Up Front" or BLUF style, and it is incredibly useful.

Sometimes, in the process of writing this summary, you might find that this process alone clarifies your thinking and you don't need all that extra detail, which is great. If you do actually need it, just put a heading over it that says "Background" or "Details" to separate it from the summary and the thing you are asking for. Depending on the work style of your team, you may even just have the summary in the message and then a link to a shared document with all the details.

Selling – How to get people to agree with you

Yes, at its core, we're talking about "selling" ideas here. For most software engineers, the idea of selling *anything* gives them an uneasy sick feeling. "Selling" conjures up images of pinky rings, expense accounts and golf. It's something those *other people do*.

This isn't about sales as a profession, though, with all those stereotypes engineers may foster about them. It is about acknowledging that all of us, no matter our role or title, end up selling quite often. When we are trying to convince people that our approach is the one they should support, or even that another proposal should not take our eye off our current priorities, that is *selling*. It might be in a formal project meeting, a sprint planning session, or even in a code review. As engineers, that type of person-to-person persuasion really is part of our job. From a strictly career perspective, selling yourself as the person who can best deliver on some business, technical or organizational need is essential to building influence.

Once we accept as truth that a "sales minded" approach is not only useful but essential, then what can we learn about selling that will help us do that better? I'm going to explain this from the perspective of a traditional sales framework. Stick with me, though, I promise to put it in the context of software engineering.

Listen to the other person and build rapport

If you've ever been on the receiving end of a bad salesperson, you know what it is like to be "sold at" rather than "listened to." If you haven't experienced this, visit a local car dealer on some Saturday and seem interested enough to attract a salesperson.

We *all* want to be listened to. It's a pretty basic human desire we all have.

Satisfy that need for the person you are trying to persuade and just listen to them express their problems and challenges they are trying to solve.

I want to be clear here that unlike that car lot salesperson, this isn't a transactional conversation. Our relationships with work colleagues are, hopefully, longer term. This isn't about using people. You should cultivate relationships sincerely and build genuine rapport that goes beyond "What do I have to do to get you into a new UI framework today?"

Now, it is fair to say that not *every* problem is equal. There are some problems that have a higher value to the business (if we are talking about work) or to a friend or partner (in our personal life). In the Xbox team, we called these "valuable problems" to separate them from the vast universe of general problems that we *could* try to solve. That phrase has always stuck with me and it is a good way to conceptually separate the things that are worth taking on right now.

Whether this other person is an executive, your manager, a customer or another engineer on your team, build a rapport with them and listen to them express their valuable problems. Don't feel like you should come up with an answer or a proposal on the spot. Focus on listening and taking notes. Use active listening techniques to confirm you are understanding them correctly.

Rather than offer off-the-cuff ideas, you might say, "Thank you for sharing that with me. I have some ideas about possible solutions but if you don't mind, I'd like to give it some more thought and maybe we could follow up on this in a few days." (or "this afternoon" or whatever timing fits the urgency of the situation)

An important part of building rapport is to understand what the other person (or team or partner company or whatever) needs to consider themselves successful in what they are trying to accomplish. And really, this could apply to your own management chain and other people on your team also, especially if your team includes other roles like marketing, operations, etc.

We need to stipulate that most people don't make the decisions they make and pursue courses of action at random or because they are "dumb" or "don't get it" (something you still hear from engineers too often). It's better to assume that they are smart, engaged people who are working toward goals and objectives for themselves and their teams and products. If, through force of will and personal charm, you got another team to agree to do something, but that thing didn't align with their business needs, in the end you shouldn't be surprised if they don't deliver it, or at least in the way you assumed they would.

What magic ways can you use to know what their goals are? I'd propose (drumroll please) that you *ask* them. Have that conversation. What does success look like for them? What would be the impacts if they changed direction? Who would need to approve the change?

Building rapport means *really* building rapport. Genuinely trying to reach a level of understanding and empathy. Yes, it takes time and effort, but if you approach it as something like a box to be checked or something that you can fake your way through, it's really not going to work.

Believe in your product – even if the product is *you*

To persuade anyone of anything, you really have to have some degree of belief in it, even if not complete zealous conviction. If you aren't convinced, you will have a hard time convincing other people. This doesn't mean you have no lingering internal doubt or questions. Nor does it mean the solution you have to believe what you are selling is *perfect* BUT you do have to believe it is the best solution available within the constraints of the project. This is true whether we're talking about a proposal for a technical architecture or that you are the best person for a new position that has caught your eye. As you come up with your pitch, it's completely OK, and even preferable, to also list out risks, gaps and potential unknowns – and you'll want to communicate these clearly as part of the pitch. It shows you have invested the time to think it through. However, you should also include how you mitigate those risks, gaps and unknowns. What steps need to be taken to fill in the blanks in that story? If it were up to you to do it, and assuming you don't have the direct ability to provide those answers, whose help would you need?

For example, let's say you work in a financial services company and you hear that a team is being formed to investigate Large Language Models (LLM) and Machine Learning (ML) and how it could be used it to reduce risks on loan products. Let's also say that you don't have any professional experience with Machine Learning. When you express your interest in this role, you might say, "I've never worked with Machine Learning, but I did a lot of the technical work on moving the Big Loan Product to a distributed architecture running in the cloud, where we've reduced costs by 35% while increasing revenue by 14%. That involved me learning a lot of new things for that project. I'm already experimenting with NumPy and TensorFlow on my own and I'm confident I can do the same thing here and deliver great results."

Understand the decision-making process

If you want to effect change, at any level, whether you are proposing a technical approach or adoption of a new process, or something more sweeping like reorganizing the teams in a division, you have to understand what the decision-making process for that thing would look like.

Who owns the decision? Who has to be involved in reaching it? Who will feel slighted if they aren't involved? It probably depends a great deal on what is being proposed.

If you are proposing changing the way your team stores data in a database that you are absolutely sure only your team's code uses, then that's probably something the team can decide – possibly some key engineers from the team, perhaps the architect if you have one. It may even be that for such a change, it is just something that group would decide and then inform other people like the team manager or director.

For all scenarios, it comes down to these key points:

- **Process:** What does the process look like for this proposal? Is it an informal matter of getting affected parties to agree it is good and to accept the work on their teams on a schedule that works? Or is it a formal process with a change control board? Does it involve budgets that need approval from some group of accounting people? Does it have legal impacts that need involvement or approval from lawyers? No matter the organization, there is almost certainly *not* a single process that works for all kinds of changes. Most likely, you are going to need to enlist help from your manager and others that they might suggest to figure out how to proceed. And that means you are first going to need to win those people over to whatever you are pitching.
- **People:** Who are the key personalities? These might be actual decision makers, or they might be respected influential people in the organization. Even if they aren't the person who owns approving the idea, you want those influential people on your side.
- **Pre-agreement:** Convince key players privately in advance. When the leaders of two countries meet in a summit to sign a treaty, those two heads of state are not sitting in that room working out the details. Rather, people from those governments have met, probably many times, to hammer out all the specifics and the

language and come to an agreement in advance of the formality of the two leaders approving it. The work we are doing in software development is usually not as complicated as that, but you can still take a lesson from that power of behind the scenes agreement. If you've identified a particular architect or senior developer as a respected influencer on the team (and I certainly hope they are), then spend time talking with them. Walk through the plan starting quite early. When possible, let them see you as accepting of their input. There will probably be more than one such influential person. If this proposal is really something you care about, invest the time to meet with all those key people separately. When things reach a point that the influencers are in agreement with the plan, tell them you will be setting up a meeting (or whatever your process requires) to finalize this and flat out ask them to support the idea in that meeting. This is the final opportunity for them to say "yes, I'm in." If they can't do that, you really can't proceed. Either you continue the discussion or, at least for now, you shelve the idea. The goal is that when you are in this final discussion, the influential people are speaking up with "I see no problem with this, we've talked about it a lot and I agree we should go ahead."

- **Close.** Whatever the process is for the decision you are trying to reach, there is some step in the process where we say "Agreed. Let's do it!" in one way or another. This is the step I referred to in the previous point where we want people to nod their heads. That doesn't mean there are no concerns and no questions. The answer might be "Let's do it, but before we start, come up with a mitigation plan for that risk about cloud data access." It is not impossible, by the way, that one of these key people could unexpectedly change sides in that final discussion. Other than knowing that is possible, and spending time getting to know these people, there's really nothing you can do about that. This is why it's good to have more than one key person on your side.

Sell the benefits

You've probably heard the old marketing adage "sell the benefits, not the features." This is why perfume ads are full of exotic and romantic imagery rather than people describing what it smells like or the easy open bottle.

You need to do the same thing.

How does your proposal solve the valuable problem? In the business world, that basically comes down to how it reduces costs or improves revenue or drives some other key metric. The fact that some technology would be cool to build and valuable experience for you or the team is not usually a key benefit by itself. The solution you propose may do those things too, which is great, but as we covered in *Principle #3 Know your business*, you need to speak the language of what is important to your organization to express the benefits.

> **Example**
> You discover your containers deployed to the cloud are consuming compute resources unnecessarily. You find an approach that you believe can optimize the code running in those virtual machines, which reduces that resource consumption. That's a fantastic story to tell and your fellow engineers will completely understand the value of it. But if you are asking management to prioritize doing this work over some other features, you may not be successful with the engineering description. In fact, you probably won't be able to convince people using that. However, if you do a little extra homework and are able to say, essentially, "I want to spend this full sprint working on optimizing the cloud compute usage and I expect this to reduce cloud compute costs for the CoolApp portion by 35%," then that is going to get some attention. If in your analysis you find it's only going to save 3%, well, then you might mention it but not try to sell it. It is

> probably not going to be very persuasive in most cases.

Of course, no work is ever free, and precious little work is as cheap as we think it will be. So, if you are going to propose investing in some work, then try to think about how that work translates into moving the needles that matter for the business - reduced operational or support costs, attracting new customers (aka "acquisition") or engaging existing customers ("engagement"), increasing profits, or whatever goals the business has prioritized (sometimes called "key performance indicators" or "KPIs"). To be able to speak to the benefits of a proposal in these terms, you need to know what overall goals are for the team, the division, the product or whatever part of the business you are in. That may sound obvious but a lot of your developer peers are not tuned into that. Many companies have regular "all hands" meetings or send out emails or otherwise share the goals for the business and progress against them on a quarterly or monthly basis. Even if that part is happening at your company (or in your division or team), it still means you have to pay attention to it at least a little bit and know where to find the information.

Once you have ensured the proposal is aligned to overall goals and you've identified the metrics related to the problem you are trying to solve, use data to illustrate the problem. If your idea is used as an experiment or fully adopted, you can later use the same type of data to compare the before and after and determine clearly if things have improved or not. Let the data do the talking.

This isn't saying you need to become the business analyst or the product owner. It's just saying you should understand what you are trying to accomplish at a higher level than just the lines of code you deliver. It's 100% OK that you don't know every detail of it. You might even start down the path of a proposal technically and then ask your lead or manager to review it and specifically ask for help in aligning it to the language and metrics of the business. *That alone* will set you apart as someone who is thinking beyond your specific set of technical tasks.

Learn from failures

What if it's a "no"?

If, after following those steps outlined in "understanding the process," you don't have agreement to proceed you usually have a choice. Is this proposal important enough, valuable enough, that you want to continue refining and revisiting? Or do you want to give up, at least for now?

Perhaps the feedback from the room is more that there are open questions or unmitigated risks, or if it just isn't high enough priority to proceed right now. If this happens, it is reasonable to ask yourself why this didn't come up in discussions with those influential people on the team. You can decide whether you want to continue to invest time to refine the proposal, answer the open questions, or reconsider the value relative to other work.

There's no shame in just accepting that it isn't going to happen. For any idea, there is a limit to what it is worth in work you are doing to continue trying to win people over. And, if the feedback is strong that this is not a good way to go, then you really need to consider the impacts continuing has on your reputation – even if you still think it's a grand idea. Ultimately, this is really just something you'll need to weigh for yourself.

Either way, I would encourage you to spend at least a few moments and do a mini-post-mortem just for yourself.

- What went well?
- What didn't go well?
- What would you do differently next time?

Gather up the notes and other artifacts from the effort and keep them. You can refer to them the next time you are proposing something. Don't lose the opportunity to learn something useful even if in the end it didn't go the way you thought it should.

I'd also encourage you to get feedback from other people involved in the process. Feedback is a gift. Hang on to the feedback they provide. It's all a learning experience.

Your career journey

"What do you want to be when you grow up?"
Ahhh, the age-old question.

To get somewhere, first you need to decide where you want to go. And when it comes to your career, you have to accept that you are in the driver's seat. You can't wait for someone else to come along and tell you what your next step should be and remind you when it is time to pursue opportunities that lead to promotions and increased responsibility. The details of exactly what this looks like and what routes are open to you differ quite a lot from one organization to another, but the central notion that your career is, quite literally, *your job* is universal. Because of all those differences, there are going to be a lot of generalities in this section. My hope is that I can at least outline the big picture possibilities and point you in a "right enough" direction that you can learn the details for your situation.

Titles don't really mean much in terms of comparing a position from one company to another. This is part of the reason for *Principle #2: Make a map.* Every time you change companies, you are going to have to apply that principle and learn what the titles mean in that organization.

Generally speaking, though, the early stages of a software engineer career look more or less like this…

All of these are "individual contributor" (IC) roles. That is, you are taking on work tasks to deliver individually as part of the team and the primary value you are bringing is in the code you are writing and the technical work you are doing. As you progress on this path, you will be expected to need less assistance in doing that work and you will have more latitude in how you do the work and perhaps what work you take on. Of course, this shouldn't be taken to mean that every software developer will do an internship (although one or more internships is, I believe, the *most valuable* part of a college or university experience) or that they will get hired as an employee in the organization where they did their internship. It would, however, be uncommon for a "campus hire" software developer to start anywhere above that Entry/Junior/Associate step.

Generally speaking, if that junior engineer delivers on their tasks, doesn't develop a reputation for causing trouble and doesn't set the data center on fire, they will most likely be promoted to a software engineer within 2 years. Frankly, if you find yourself at that level and you've been reasonably delivering level appropriate results at the same company when you hit 3 years, you probably need to be looking elsewhere for your next step.

As a software engineer and senior software engineer, you will not only be delivering on your own work, but you'll have a responsibility to help grow the overall capability and level of the team. You'll be contributing actively to design discussions and investigations of operational incidents. You'll be providing meaningful and effective feedback in code reviews. And you will probably be mentoring interns and helping new hires come up to speed and doing more advising of junior team members. You won't actually be managing them in an org chart sense, but you are providing important leadership. As you grow professionally, keep in mind that these duties outside of writing code aren't *extra* work. They really represent an important and core part of your job.

As you move into the senior role, you will become more involved in *how* the team executes on plans. You'll probably be asked your opinion more about how the team should be structured and how it should operate. You'll be more involved in interviewing candidates for hiring and you may be involved in managing the functional work of contractors and other resources. All of this brings you to a decision point for your career and what comes next. It comes down to whether or not you want to manage people. As I mentioned in the introduction, it isn't required that you manage people to advance well in your software engineering career, and if you don't feel drawn to managing people, then you definitely should *not* do it. It won't work out well for you, the people you reluctantly manage or, really, the company as a whole.

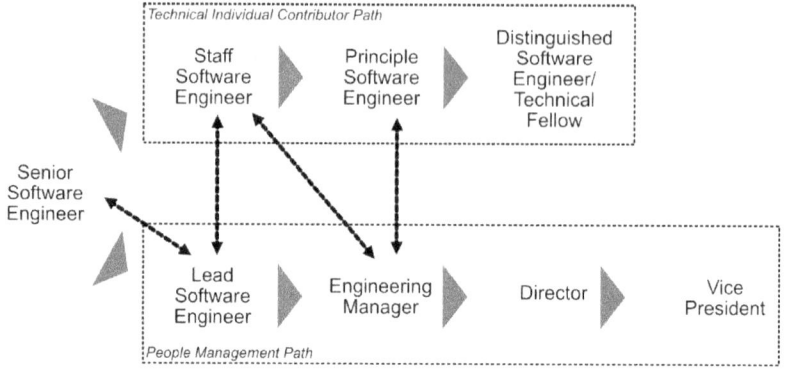

These increasingly senior IC roles are filling an important leadership role. Those on the management track are going to consult them and probably be quite accepting of their technical guidance. People in these IC roles work on progressively the hardest technical challenges facing the organization. They will still be writing some code, but they will also be driving technical decisions at the architectural level more and more. They will also have an important voice in *how* the organization executes technical tasks. If you want to reach the principal and staff engineer ranks, you need to spend less time in front of your code editor and much more time talking to customers, designers, product owners, your current peers and the principal and staff engineers who would be your peers. You will need to develop skills that emphasize raising the productivity and quality of the team as a whole, not just yourself. This means defining practices and standards, reviewing, advising and mentoring as a much larger part of your day than it has been to this point in your career.

Now let's walk down the management side, starting with a Lead Software Engineer.
There is definitely no hard rule for the size of team a "lead" will lead, but the "two pizza team" has become a common

benchmark. You might also hear it called a feature team, scrum team or pod.

In this Lead role, you will be responsible not just for the work getting done and technical leadership, both of which continue to be an important part of your job description, but also in personnel management and employee career responsibilities – like regular one-on-one discussions, goal setting, performance reviews, etc. And you are still responsible for being deeply engaged technically and need to be able to represent the work the team is doing and be accountable for it. You'll be considering key questions as you work with the team to deliver, such as:

- Is this solution delivering the right capabilities the customer needs *now*?
- Is the design of the system able to reasonably expand for future plans? Maybe we have a modest set of deliverables for a version 1, but can we deliver version 2 without rebuilding everything?
- What are the risks of the planned approach? And how can we mitigate them?
- Have we considered scaling and cost factors so the system works for the customer and the business as the user base grows?

These additional responsibilities will likely impact the amount of individual work you will deliver. That's not a failure on your part, it's just the math involved in hours in the day. A good expectation is that you will spend about ¼ to ½ a day per week for every direct report you manage. This isn't because you will literally spend that much time per week engaging with each person, though there is some of that, but you'll have other people management-related meetings and tasks that require your time and attention and it ends up averaging out to that figure. As you move into a lead position, don't be surprised when your number of code check-ins goes down, often *way* down.

You should consider carefully whether you want to manage people, rather than just viewing it as the next logical step in a career. A 2023 UK study by the Chartered Management Institute (CMI) found that "82% of workers entering management positions have not had any formal management and leadership training." The same study referred to "accidental managers," meaning people who really didn't have a passion for management but were placed in those positions based on tenure, popularity or other reasons. Embarking on a management path when you don't want to actually do it is a disservice to yourself and very much to those you would be poorly managing.

As you continue along this track, your value rapidly becomes less and less about any code that you personally write and more about the code you *cause to be written* by the other engineers on your team. You'll be more involved in structuring the teams to deliver on business objectives, ensuring the team members are growing and improving and that the hiring process is working effectively. And, yes, dealing with people-centered issues. Who isn't working effectively? Who are positive and negative influences on the team? Etc.

An important aspect of this part of the path is that there is usually room to go back and forth, up to a point. It is more common to switch between the IC and Management tracks relatively earlier on. For example, it's quite common to go back and forth between lead and senior software engineer roles as the needs of the organization evolve over time. It would be very uncommon (almost unheard of) for a Director, VP or CTO to switch over to the IC side, or for a Distinguished Engineer to move to management at that stage of their career.

Managing your own career

When it comes to the important topic of moving your career forward and getting promoted, there are some examples, such as government, certain union or collective bargaining arrangements, or regions with specific regulatory requirements, where there are systems based on seniority, tenure, formal examinations or other clear steps, but those are exceptions. If you work in a situation like this, you really need to understand the process and the requirements for promotion. This may take some digging but your manager, your peers and your Human Resources team can provide valuable information.

In most organizations where software engineers work, there are not an absolute set of steps and defined requirements for promotion. You'll often hear in employer training materials something to the effect that "each employee needs to be responsible for their own career," but what does that actually mean?

This is really just saying that, as I said in the introduction, you can't just sit quietly and do good work and wait for your manager to notice and promote you. You will likely be sitting quietly for a very long time. That CMI study referenced above, reporting on the "accidental" and poorly prepared managers is a big reason why you need to *own* your career. Think about what that means for you. This data suggest that you simply can't rely on your manager to sort all this out for you. Now, if you happen to have a solid manager or even a great one, so much the better. It is still *your* career we are talking about here and you need to take hold of it. If you can get some support and advocacy from your managers along the way, so much the better.

Your manager can be a key part of the process. An effective manager will help point you to the information you need to plan your steps and help gather feedback that helps you understand how other people see your strengths and areas where you still need to grow. You definitely should foster a positive relationship with your manager. **BUT** you need to do your part and inform yourself to participate well in those kinds of discussions.

Think about these things:

- **Professionally, what are your goals?**
  If your real goal is to learn what you can from this job and then quit and go work for Huge Company X as a VP of Engineering, that's fine, though you might want some other version of that story to tell your manager when they ask you. The important thing is **you** need to understand for yourself what your real goals are.
- **What do you lack to get to that goal?**
  You'll want to do some honest soul-searching about where you are relative to achieving that goal. There may be 300 things you need to become great at to get that VP of Engineering job, but what are the *next* two or three you are going to work on? By the way, peer feedback can be one useful tool to help find those gaps.
- **How can you close that gap?** What are the expectations of your current position and level and what are the expectations for the next step if you were to stay in the same company?
  This goes back to the discussion under *Principle #2: Make a map.*

- **Understand expectations for your current and next level.** As a manager, this is the first homework assignment I give team members who tell me they want to get promoted. "OK," I say, "to what? And how are the expectations for that level different from where you are right now?" If you come into that conversation with your manager having already done that work, right away you give the impression of someone with their act together.
- **What do you need from your manager?** What do you want out of that relationship? Are you looking for help with those skill gaps? Are you looking for direct and candid feedback? Are you looking for specific opportunities? Have regular one-on-one sessions with your manager and let them know these are things you want. It's hard to be on either side of that discussion when there is really just silence so you end up talking about tasks status to fill the time. There is a fine line here to be sure. Don't be the team member who seems to care more about climbing ladders than doing the work today. You need to strike a reasonable balance and show your leader you are willing to give them what they need in exchange for support in what you want.

A lot of this is very much core to the idea of building a good working relationship with your manager. Team members who do these things, who communicate well with their colleagues while also doing solid work are, unfortunately, just really rare. When you picked up this book, and others like it, you took a major step in managing your own career. It really just means being an active participant, rather than waiting for things to happen for you.

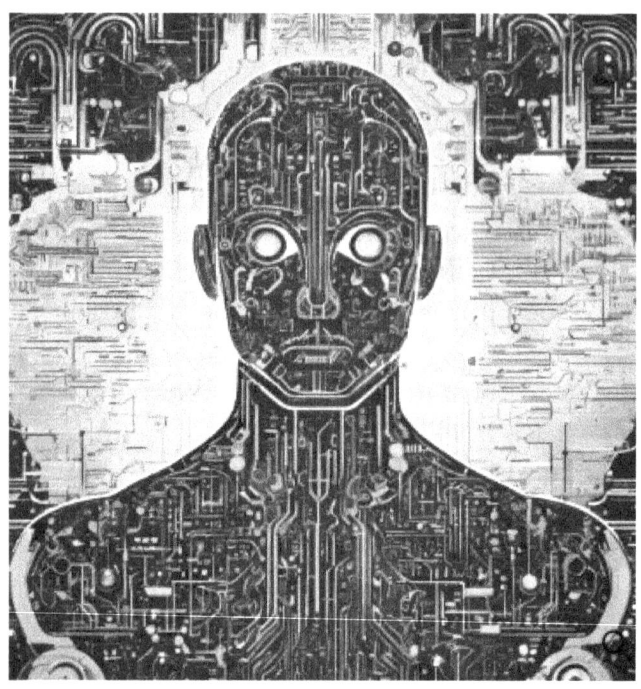

What about AI?

Let's face it. The presence of Large Language Model (LLM) Artificial Intelligences tools like ChatGPT comes up in just about every conversation with developers. What do these things mean for their careers? Are we all going to be out of work? It's such a dominant topic, it feels like something that any developer career book in 2024 needs to take head on and address in some way.

Bad news first. Yes, there are most definitely going to be job impacts in our field as a result of AI. We've already seen some early stages of some of those impacts.

There are a variety of estimates and statistics, but to take just one, Evans Data Corporation (EDC) there are about 27 million software developers in the world, spanning everything from web page scripting to low level operating system coders. And that number has grown by about 3% per year for the past several years. That total is a little more than the entire population of Australia, or a couple million less than the entire US state of Texas.

This will sound brutal, but you probably know this is true from your own experience. Of those millions of developers, there are quite a lot who honestly aren't adding a lot of value in their role and are operating at the very lower edge of knowledge and skill. There are developers who drive a lot of their daily work either by repeatedly doing the same basic set of things, or who rely heavily on web searches and tools like Stack Overflow. That's not to say that the rest of us are re-inventing the wheel and never using those resources, but there needs to be a balance in terms of what we, individually, are bringing to the table. "Copy and Paste" devs are the most at risk as this trend unfolds.

You can almost view the current generation of AI tools as just a more efficient step (or half step) ahead of a web search, so what are we to do?

Now the good news. You can protect yourself through this period of change by doing a few things.

1) **Learn how to appropriately and efficiently use AI tools for your work.** Part of this is learning how to craft the right prompts. The emerging term for this is "prompt engineering," which basically means asking the questions in the right ways to get the most useful result. Just like you know how to use your other tools like your code editor, your source control system and your build system, learn how to use this new tool. Another aspect of this, though, is understanding any policies your company may have around using these tools. Part of the problem can be that the prompts you submit, including code snippets in them, generally become part of the training set for these tools. And that can result in Intellectual Property leakage. In short, treat it as if you were posting something on the public internet. If your organization would care about that, then you need to know those rules.

2) **Add genuine value.** This one is really the key, and yes, this is really the same advice all the other principles and topics in this book have been driving toward. Wherever you are working, you need to understand the business you are in and align the work you are delivering with the goals of the overall business, your division, your team, etc.

3) **Keep your eyes open.** Don't ignore change in our field, and don't beat the drum of fear with your colleagues. Be the person who is able to explain how these things work. Experiment on your own. Be part of the change rather than trying to pretend it isn't happening – and that goes for more than just AI. Good engineers should always be experimenting with new tools and techniques, with AI tools being a specific example of that.

I'll add one more thing. In the section *Be a sharer, not a hoarder,* I talk about the idea of "brown bag sessions." Machine Learning and AI is a great example of a new and interesting topic that would present a good opportunity for you to lead such a discussion. You can give a short demo of AI powered dev tools like OpenAI's ChatGPT or Microsoft's Copilot, just to mention two, followed by discussion of how this could work for real life dev projects. Like all such sessions, you don't need to cast yourself as an expert, just as an interested party who wants to spur thinking and conversation.
You might also try to create a group of engineers to explore AI in the context of the work your organization does. What implications does it have on your coding standards? How do you manage the risks of Intellectual Property leakage that I mentioned? Can engineers provide a voice to the legal team to help them understand how these systems work? All of those things are opportunities for you to not only help yourself and the engineering team grow, but also for you to demonstrate visible impact and grow your influence.

Mentors

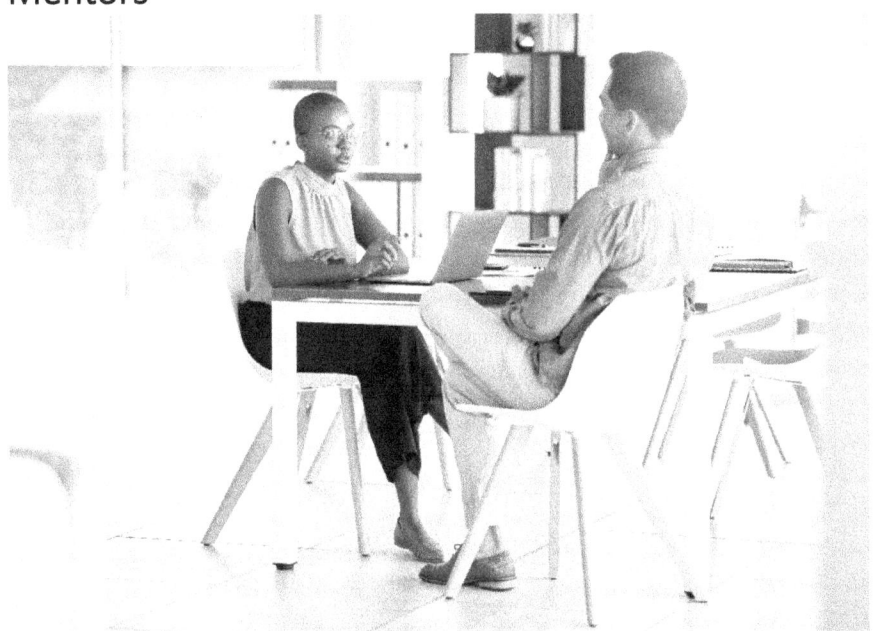

This is a difficult section for me to write. I've been a mentor for several people. Some have become very successful, some have struggled and left the industry completely. With all of those people, I feel like we had productive relationships and I'm still in touch with many of them years later.

On the other side, I've tried to have a mentor relationship for myself at times, but just in total transparency, it's never been a useful part of my career path. Yes, I've gotten valuable insights from senior people and we've had trusting relationships, but these have tended to be more around short-term direct guidance with specific problems. I had sort of a problem-based transactional relationship. I'd say that was indeed mentoring, but it isn't what you typically think of when someone says "mentor."

There has been lots written about mentoring and how to make it work for you. While it's tempting, because it feels like something that belongs in a career book like this, I'm not going to try to recast any of that as my own thinking. Classic mentoring hasn't met a need for me but that doesn't mean it won't be greatly helpful for you.

Here are a few basic thoughts around mentoring to get you thinking.

- **You want the perspective distance provides.** Don't expect your manager to be your mentor. Yes, if you have a great manager, you are going to learn a lot from them and you should. That's not the same as a mentor. You want a mentor who brings fresh eyes and different thinking. Definitely not your manager or someone in your team. Preferably someone not even in your same business unit or part of the company. Sometimes they don't even work in the same company. It's ok if they don't know the details of the project you are on – it's not about a person who can do code reviews for you.

- **You need to make the investment to prepare.** When you have a mentor and you are going to meet with them, *you* need to be the one to prepare the agenda. You are the one seeking guidance, so that is only fair. Let's say you typically have a 1-hour monthly meeting with your mentor. One is coming up this week and you don't really have anything you want to talk about. Maybe you should cancel. Or, maybe you should just trim it to 20 or 30 minutes and grab a cup of coffee or have lunch together. Don't tie the person up for an hour without an agenda. And don't just make your agenda whatever the freshest thing that happened this week. Think longer term and deeper.

- **It's not a gripe session.** This is probably one of the biggest mistakes people make in mentor relationships. A mentor isn't really your therapist, your hair stylist or your drinking buddy. Now, let's consider an example where you are having a problem communicating effectively with a team member. Then as you reflect on that you see that maybe there is a pattern you've had in difficult communications with other people. Now we have something interesting to explore with a mentor. "Hey I have noticed I sometimes have a problem talking productively with this kind of person. I'm hoping you can help me see my blind spots and get better at that."

- **Don't make it weird.** Pay attention to social cues from your mentor and don't make them uncomfortable. I remember a particular person I mentored at Microsoft. We had a good and productive relationship. This person was very academic in his approach to things and one aspect of that is that when we would talk, he would literally transcribe everything I was saying in a notebook. Not taking highlight notes, but like a court stenographer. As a result, we had two kinds of barriers between us. There is the obvious physical barrier of his paper notebook (same would go for a laptop or tablet) that he had his eyes focused on. The second was that I really didn't like the idea of this total written record of everything I said, because (true self-awareness here) sometimes I say stuff that may be off-the-cuff or maybe a little crazy when taken out of context. In exploring this with him, I found this is how he took notes in all his conversations and he'd had negative feedback on it before. This gave us some things to talk about, including alternate strategies he might consider.
- **It's not forever.** This doesn't need to be a long-term relationship. Very little we do at work is actually a permanent, immutable decision. It's 100% OK to have a mentor for a while and then end that relationship and start a new one as your needs change. That doesn't mean you never talk to that person again, just that that part of the relationship has run its course.

Many large companies have established mentoring programs. No matter what your preconceived notions about mentoring are, if you have access to these programs, give it a fair shot.

Programs like this are definitely one of the benefits of working in a large organization.

If you've tried mentoring before and not found it useful, give it another go as your career situation changes. Maybe it will never be the right thing for you, but it's good to have it in your toolbox as a possibility.

Being an engaged, productive team member

As humans, there are just some techniques and approaches to keep in mind when trying to work productively with other people and get things done. There are elements of communication, emotion and psychology that come into play whenever two or more people are engaged in any effort. This section isn't about tricks to play on other people to get your way. It's really about tools for you to just get along better so that you can be more successful in what you are trying to do and be seen by others as a good person to have around.

There is some truth to the idea that it would be really nice if we all just came to work and did our things and by doing that work, things would just work out. Reality intrudes, though. Even people who consider themselves coldly rational are still driven by all those irrational, human factors.

Manage your own priorities

Lots of us keep to-do lists. Maybe we keep it in an app, maybe it's written on a whiteboard next to our desk. Or maybe sticky notes stuck to the side of our monitor. And maybe we have had some success with those methods. I've even worked with people who had multiple to-do lists in multiple tools and documents, which, not surprisingly, doesn't work at all. What's the problem with these? Why don't to-do lists work better? Really, the problem is that the lists grow faster than items are removed. We end up with an imposing out of control list that is just such a huge ball of work that it can make us feel hopeless to even look at it. It stops driving our action just from the mass of it. When it is beyond hope, maybe we will just start *a new list*!

When I was a teenager, someone taught me a technique I've used ever since. It's so simple I didn't even know it had a name until much later. That name, by the way, is the "Ivy Lee Method," named for the man who created or at least evangelized it, in the early 20th century. There are some fun

107

stories, which may or may not be true, about how it became popular. I'll leave that for you and Google to sort out.

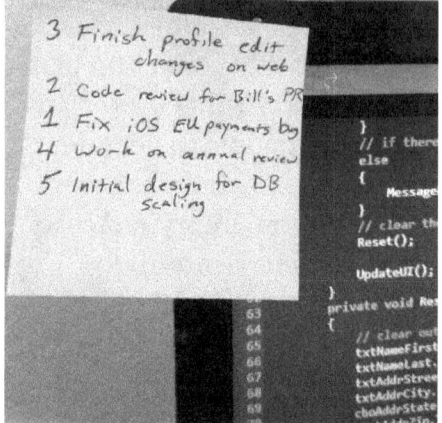 

The Ivy Lee Method is also a to-do list. There are three keys to why it works.

- **It's a short list.** You should never have more than six items on the list. It's not *everything* in the universe of your to-do's. It's just the most immediate things. You can decompose it any way that feels appropriate to you. Probably no two people have the same granularity to their list items. It probably won't just be the same as your list of project tasks from Jira, though. It might be a breakdown of the current task you are working on plus things like "prepare for Friday campus candidate interview panel," etc.
- **Freshen it every day.** Every day, at the end of your day, look at your list. Cross off whatever you accomplished. Add whatever near-term tasks have popped up. Prioritize the items on your list as a simple stack rank of one to six. If you are keeping the list on paper, now jot it onto a clean one with the items in priority order. Now you won't start the next day trying to figure out what to do because you already did that –

in what is generally the less productive part of your day.

- **Focus on the top priority.** When you come in the next day and are ready to work, focus on your #1 item. If you work all day diligently and still don't complete that item, you can still say to yourself "I spent my time today on my most important thing." When that item is done, you move to the next priority in the list. If other truly high priority fires appear, that's OK. Just deal with what you need to, but don't mistake the merely urgent for the truly important just because people are freaking out about it. Make sure it really is more important than the priority you were working on.

This is *your* list. You don't need to review it with other people. If you have a priority on your list that is to prep for an interview for your next job, or go to lunch with a friend, that is absolutely fine. It's a tool just for you.

That's it. It's really more of a habit than some amazing technique in its own right. As with all habits, the power really comes from doing it day in and day out.

How and when to say "no"

I may as well just say it. Learning to say "no" is a key superpower in your career success. All other things being equal, it is a key differentiator over time between those people who achieve what they consider enduring "success" in our industry and those who struggle or rise and then burn out. There seems no shortage of people who want us to do work tasks that are important, maybe even genuinely essential, to them. And they may be 100% correct in asking. It's very easy to say no to bad ideas. (And, by the way, those who say "there are no bad ideas" clearly haven't been doing this for very long.) The challenge comes when the task or idea is a good and worthy thing to do…but it isn't aligned to our priorities and goals *right now*. This is one of the reasons it is so important that we (and by "we" I mean ICs, leads, managers, teams etc.) need to be clearly aligned and agreed on what our priorities and goals are. It's not a forever decision. We might adjust them from one release to the next. We can even adjust them for the current release, although the reasons to do that need to be really clear, or we end up just bouncing around all the time chasing constantly changing priorities.

You might be thinking, "Hey, saying 'No' makes people mad. I don't want to make people mad at me."
Well, yes. That can be true, but what **definitely** causes people to get upset is when work is agreed to and doesn't happen. That often has all kinds of downstream impacts that ripple across other teams. It can impact release dates, contractual obligations, marketing and the company stock price.
A poorly thought through "yes" today can cause much more pain later if it proves unrealistic or otherwise unattainable. Saying "no" is a side effect of having priorities and having priorities is an admission, if you will, that there is an infinite amount of work we could do and a finite ability to actually do it, and do it to the level of quality we need.

I'm going to say the quiet part out loud here. Most of us in software engineering are just not great at estimating the real full cost of work. I've said for years that if you ask most devs how long some task is going to take, the first number that they'll answer is really "the amount of time to kind of get this sort of working…on my machine." With some additional probing and prompting, they get to a number that includes all the necessary code reviews, tests, whatever documentation and so on. It's not because they aren't smart. Part of this is because a lot of our work includes a healthy amount of "I've-never-done-this-before-but-I'll-figure-it-out" and because most of us, whether we are new to the industry or well experienced, somehow, manage to stay hopelessly optimistic (while also being bitingly cynical) about what we're doing. We end up working later hours, skipping lunches, and working weekends to get things all wrapped up before the end of a sprint or a push to prod or whatever milestone is involved. This is just more or less the natural state. If you say "yes" to additional work, that implies we are now *planning* to spend that additional time that in many cases we're already on-track to spend on *unplanned* work.

It is critical to understand, internalize and believe that

Predictability > Heroics

We all want to be the person who saves the day. We hope we'll be recognized and rewarded for it and this "mad scientist coder" image is deep in our culture. It's just a terrible way to run a business. What happens when the hero is on vacation or out sick or just wants to go water skiing on Saturday?

An interesting thing is that this heroic pattern worked better in the older days of software where there was a ship cycle that might be one or several years and the team ramped up in intensity (and often in size) over that span, released the software on a shiny CD and then settled back into planning and design and took a breath before starting again. Today, we are in the Agile and Continuous Integration/Continuous Delivery (CI/CD) worlds of very frequent releases and updates. We can't go backward, but we can't run our engine at racetrack intensity constantly by trying to apply those old models to our world now.

We need to accept it is better for us as individuals and teams and all the way up through the business, and to our customers, to predictably set schedules and stick to them. And that means we have to say "no" at the right times and in productive ways.

When we consider our list of tasks, as engineers we are probably thinking of our technical tasks. The code we will write for sure. Maybe we think of design reviews and getting PRs all the way through the workflow gates. But we can't forget all our *other* the tasks that come with the *other* part of your job. Interviewing candidates, mentoring interns, providing peer feedback, working on patent applications, even staying caught up on messaging channels. All of that is also real work and it all requires time. You should consider the totality of the work that you honestly have in front of you when you are deciding whether you can take on an additional work item, or whether you should say no – either to that additional item or to some of the lower priority other things you are doing.

We need to be open to applying the same thinking to taking on those tasks. If you are swamped with interviews because recruiting thinks you do a great job at it, you may need to get them to pull back a little. If you are overwhelmed with peer feedback requests because you give thoughtful, clear feedback, you may need to be more selective in which of those you respond to.

Many flavors of "no"

There are many ways to say "no." Often you innately understand why you are turning down a request. It's important, though, for you to be able to communicate to the person asking for the work why it is you are refusing what to them is probably a sensible desire. This does two important things. First, it makes you seem like a team player who is actually thinking things through and not just being a jerk. Second, communicating the reason can open the door to useful conversations, again keeping things on a professional and productive level.

You want to be seen as not just dismissing things out of hand. You want to be clear you are focused on the best outcome for the project or product overall. You are essentially playing the "transparency" card here. You are saying, in some form:

1) I understand you need this.
2) Here is the work I'm already committed to do.
3) Unless something here changes, I can't do the thing you want until…

The actual conversation might look something like this: "I don't think I can give this task the attention it would need right now. Here are my tasks and priorities that I'm working on. For me to take this on, I'd need your help in adjusting these other expectations with my manager and other stakeholders. Would you be willing to help make that case?" As you can see, this isn't going to be the end, just the beginning of the discussion. If you are a more junior person on the team, you should definitely enlist the support of your manager on this. Ideally, they will just take the job of pushing back on this from you. In fact, depending on the workplace dynamic and relative power structure, they may be in a better position to just give a hard "NO!" and have that be it. Whatever happens, if someone other than your manager is trying to get you to take on work, even if that is the CTO or other executive, you need to make sure your manager is in the loop on it and part of the discussion. And even if you are the lead or manager of the team, you should at least inform your manager that this is going on.

Here are some additional ways you might frame the "no."

What you say	What it means
Is there any room to reduce the scope of your request?	What you are looking for here is the true minimum viable implementation. Is there some subset of truly essential work that is less than the initial request?

This is not aligned with current priorities.	I/we are working on the things that align to the vision and goals as they have been communicated to us. We can't do this thing because it isn't more important than any of the other work we are doing. And we don't see any near-term prospect of making room for it. This invites the conversation about either how you are not seeing something correctly or the overall priorities have indeed changed and you need to re-evaluate the things you are focusing on.
We can consider for our next <increment of work> (release, update, quarter, whatever).	I/we can't do it right now, but here is when we *can* do the work in a future increment. This invites a conversation about timing of getting the work done.
We'd need *X* from you to do this.	This is all about the exploration of alternatives. I/we can't do this on our own right now because of other work. BUT if your team can do *X* or arrange for someone to commit to *X*, we could make room to do this work. This opens the door to a discussion about what would need to be true to allow your team to do the work. Is there work that the requesting team can do that is on your plan, which would then let you do this work? Can they do the work on what they are requesting if you or your team could consult and advise but not own the code? Does the requester have the ability to convince another team to take on some set of work from you to allow you to then do the thing they are asking? Make sure, of course, whatever other team is being promised is in the loop on this conversation and commits to their part of the work.

Never.	It's not a good idea. It's in no way aligned with our current or foreseeable vision and plan. Unless something were to radically change, we don't *ever* see this happening and we just want to kill the discussion.
	Basically, this is the equivalent of you being a jet engine company and someone trying to get you to do the work to build a frozen yogurt machine because research shows many jet engine customers also eat frozen yogurt.
	In this case, you are not inviting a conversation at all, unless it is to show that you have radically misunderstood the request.

Here are two examples in the form of my own experiences in saying no to people at different times in my career and in very different ways, followed by my own critique of my performance.

Jon puts his foot firmly in his mouth

I'm including this story to show that we all learn and grow over time.

For a period of time before the Internet took off, Microsoft Automap had a rich array of content. All kinds of great information about parks and trails and historic things along your route, all written by real human writers. I was leading a small team of contract developers at the time working on tools for this editorial team.

They would have feature requests and we did a lot of them, but one set of work in particular I pushed back on. They had a way to do this in the existing tools that was a little more labor intensive and they wanted it automated. We were stretched very thin and I said "no," citing the workaround. After a few days of discussion, they invited me to the editorial team meeting. They reiterated the request and I demonstrated the workaround. Conversation turned to the cost of them using

> the existing workaround versus us automating it in our tools. And then it happened…
> I said, matter-of-factly, "You're comparing expensive developer time to cheaper editor time. English majors are a dime a dozen, just hire more of them." (By some accounts, I actually suggested they might find these additional English majors on street corners around the nearby University of Washington.)
> I looked around at the shocked faces of a *room full of English majors*.

OK, not proud of it. Not well handled. I wish I'd said it differently.

I'll add that this comment was so infamous, that *to this day* some of the same people who were in that room still mention this when I see them.

In the end, we didn't build that feature and we're still friends. It was a rough crowd back then so I'm sure this isn't the worst thing any of us heard in a meeting on that team, but it was pretty bad.

This was very early in my career and very early in working inside such a big team. Clearly, I didn't do a good job with this.

First of all, the right way to handle this would have been to *not* have this conversation in the meeting with the full editorial team. The person who invited me was kind of setting me up to make it more difficult for me to refuse. In hindsight, I should have listened to the feedback and just said I would get back to them. I should have followed up by scheduling a meeting with the manager of the editorial team, walked through our existing committed roadmap and why our priorities mapped out the way they did and used that as the basis for saying "no." Even if I wanted to get into the relative resource costs, hopefully in a more civil way, that was really for a smaller lead to lead conversation.

But I did learn from it, and lots of people got a good story out of it.

> **Saying no to a bug fix**
>
> I mentioned the old way of shipping software with multi-year release cycles. The most extreme example of that for me personally was on the Microsoft SQL Server team. While I came to the team with a lot of experience shipping quite a few products, because of the long release cycle for SQL Server, it was pretty common for people to have joined the team as their first software engineering job, worked on it for a couple years and risen to be a lead – but never yet shipped a product.
>
> We were coming up on a Beta release and I was looking through our bug database. There was a *very* minor, low priority user interface bug that had a very clear workaround. I could see we were just **never** going to fix it.
>
> I resolved it as "Won't Fix" and added a comment.
>
> Within 10 minutes a breathless test lead burst into my office and said "You meant to mark this as 'Won't fix' just for the Beta, right?"
>
> I said, "No, I mean never, ever."
>
> There was a minor freak-out followed by the words "We have to fix it! It's a defect!"
>
> I said, as gently as I could, "Look, I know it sucks, but this bug is really nothing. By the time we actually release, you'll see, we will be 'won't fixing" way worse bugs than this. Some of them will keep you up at night. This isn't one."
>
> It worked out exactly that way and, almost two decades later, it was still the right time to say "no."

This one went pretty well, I think. This doesn't mean the other person was happy about it, people don't like to be refused. By this time, I had a lot more experience with large teams and frankly just a lot more experience shipping big complicated software. It was the right decision, it didn't come back again later and at least from my perspective, it was a teachable moment for that lead about the realities of the tradeoffs we make every day in this business.

What if you can't say "no"

Unfortunately, there are some organizations that will simply not accept "no" from any of the engineering team. Maybe they view software engineers as perpetual "sandbaggers" who overstate risks and estimates so they can goof off. Maybe the managers have just retained an outdated culture of "I'm the boss!" and there's no room for collaboration and productive discussion.

You may even have situations where the person refusing to take "no" for an answer *is your manager*. If that happens, the best you can hope for is a conversation about priorities. Something like "If this is now priority 1, is there anything on this list that is now out of the plan? Or can we reduce the scope of any of these things?"

I know places like this exist. I've regularly spoken with very dedicated and capable developers who feel they are stuck in them.

When you reach a point where you are truly (and only you can judge "truly") mired in dysfunction and toxicity, it's probably time to flip forward to *The breaking point* section and start making other plans for your career.

Be a sharer, not a hoarder

Our work in software engineering is fundamentally built on knowledge and information. Knowledge of dev tools, debugging techniques, optimizations for scalability or performance, understanding of frameworks and APIs, and, importantly, knowledge of how other parts of the systems work and how our pieces interface with them. Sadly, we still encounter people who seem to feel that they are protecting their own value in an organization by deliberately hoarding knowledge of these details, especially internal details and histories of how things work and why they are the way they are.

Please don't do that.

Modern software development is a team sport. We still value those heroes and miracle workers on our teams, but not because they are keeping things to themselves. This actually harms a team's ability to deliver. What's more, for those people holding tight to arcane secret knowledge, that approach doesn't actually give them the job security and power the way they think it might.

Now, to be fair, there is another reason information isn't shared in a systematic way. Quite simply, it takes work to capture this intelligence and we are usually all pretty busy. There are whole companies, products and consultancies built around knowledge management. It's a hard problem.

It's totally natural and fine that the team members have different areas of expertise. This sharing isn't about making everyone interchangeable. A baby step in this process is at least knowing who are the experts on which parts and writing that down somewhere. Building some redundancy or "bench depth" on vital areas is also important, but you have to start somewhere.

There are two things you as an individual contributor can do to help this situation:

- Adopt the mindset of being an information sharer, not an information hoarder.
- When you are scoping a task and thinking of story points or other estimation for it, consider the time to capture some form of basic documentation for it. Basically, treat it just like testing or other non-code work that goes with a task. This doesn't need to be some *War and Peace* formal design document. Even a page of notes about what is going on at a system level is better than not having it. And we're not talking about explaining the *code*. This is about capturing the intent, dependencies and especially the assumptions you have made. Capturing a few basic bullet points is better than some perfect and complete document that doesn't exist.

There are additional steps that the broader team can take together and any team member should be bringing these ideas up and working to build energy and support for them.

Weeklogs

When I was at Unity Technologies, they had an interesting culture of teams sending out "weeklogs." This is a GREAT idea. Unfortunately, as the company grew, this habit eroded in both the number of teams doing it and the quality of what they were sending.

The point is not to create the dreaded "status report" or to duplicate a Sprint retrospective or standup. We had an email alias that everyone in the company was on and a folder and filter for these emails was preset for everyone. Anyone can read them, but the intended audience is really other engineers, program and product managers.

The goal is *not* to make the reader an expert on your plan or the history or the business case or any of that. The goal is to give a little context, catch attention with some visuals and point them to the people and places where they can find more.

This is what should be in a good weeklog:

- Name of the project.
- A sentence or two summarizing what it does.
- Key contacts. Usually the dev lead, the TPM and product manager, but can also include design lead or other important people.
- Links to where you store your stuff – Jira, Sharepoint, shared folders, etc.
- The next important date you are working toward – maybe an alpha or beta or the next significant release or conference when you are doing a demo.
- OK, this next part is important. You need to show people what *cool* stuff you've done or have in progress. Pictures are golden here. Screenshots, mockups, 30 second videos, pictures of a block diagram for a new API from a whiteboard.

That's it. I used to tell the people I was working with that if they spend more than 30 minutes on a weeklog email they are either trying to say way too much or they aren't as in-touch with the project as they should be. It should be very low friction. There's nothing in here about how many devs you

121

> have, how many story points you delivered, no justification of time spent, no projection of revenue if you can just get it released. None of that. This is 80% tech talk and 20% advertising for your team.

> I encourage you to try this approach, even if you are also required to do some other status reporting or whatever. The cost is low and potential benefit is high.

Treat knowledge capture as part of the work

I touched on this as something individual team members can consider when estimating work, but it is even better when the *team* and the *whole organization* internalizes capturing information and storing it in a reasonable, searchable way as part of the work. "But this will slow us down!" will be the complaint from some. Yes, maybe that is true, but so does testing and validation and I hope we aren't tossing that out the window. The key is to do it in a measured, sustainable and pragmatic way. Remember, this isn't about writing a 30-page design document. Two pages, a phone picture of a couple diagrams on a whiteboard, a couple paragraphs, a document where you paste the Slack discussion threads about the work – any of that is way better than what lots of projects are doing now.

60-80% of the work done on software is spent in maintaining it. Far more than is spent writing it originally. By capturing some basic information about why a component does things the way it does will pay dividends (and *save* time) for years into the future typically. The future you will be grateful.

Managing your manager

What does it mean to "manage your manger"? Why would *you* manage your *manager*? This isn't about manipulation or mind tricks. Your manager has a job they need to do. They are under as much (or more) pressure to deliver on their tasks for their manager as you feel for your daily work. Managing your manager is really about establishing clarity in your relationship with your manager and to generally make managing you less work for your manager. People that do this tend to have more career success. There's no doubt that sometimes you actually *need* support from your manager when you have something going on in your personal or work life. There's no shame in that; providing this kind of help is part of a manager's job.

Think of your relationship with your manager as a bank account. You are making deposits into that account by being forthcoming with information without it having to be pulled out of you, by doing the things you commit to do and supporting your manager in achieving the goals and milestones they need to hit. You make withdrawals from that account when you need their support like some schedule flexibility because of a personal problem, missing the completion date for a task, or needing support (sometimes you hear this called "air cover") in a dispute or conflict. You want to keep the balance in that relational account as high as you can. Managers think of different people as "easy" or "hard" to manage. An easy to manage person is not a push-over who just does what they are told. Rather they are keeping their value high and helping the manager keep their *own* value high as well, while removing mysterious unsaid expectations. All of this is central to building a mutually trusting relationship where you and your manager are collaborating to help one another achieve your respective goals while meeting the overall goals of the organization as a whole. You want to be an ally for your manager so they will be your ally in return.

The first step in managing your manager is to understand what you should expect your manager to be doing. In most, but not all, organizations, your manager has, at a minimum, two responsibilities that involve you.

1) They manage your day-to-day task work. Who is doing what? When is it due? What progress is being made? We can call this *functional management*. Some of this functional management also involves other people that may not actually report to your manager. People like project managers, scrum masters, product owners, designers, and the like. All of those different roles can impact what is being worked on and when that work can happen. It's important to note that these indirect management relationships will still *almost always* be providing feedback to your actual manager, so don't treat them casually just because they aren't directly over you in the org chart.

2) They take care of *people management* responsibilities, such as reviews and feedback, one-on-one and team meetings, ensuring company policies and expectations are communicated and enforced, and generally all the non-task specific organizational work.

I say "most" because there are cases where these two core responsibilities may be divided between different individuals. There are some companies who use (or have used in the past) a separate people manager who may manage a very large number of people – sometimes dozens. This turns that role into someone who is handling the "paperwork" but may not really have much of an idea what these people are doing for their daily work. I am not a fan of this model, but it does exist. In such a case, there is another individual handling only the functional management tasks. There is supposed to be communication between the two managers, but it is a good idea for you to keep your people manager updated on what you are working on and what value you are delivering. Don't just assume they know.

The next step in managing your manager is to understand what they are trying to achieve. What are the goals and Objectives and Key Results (OKRs) that they are responsible to deliver? What metrics or key performance indicators (KPIs) do they pay attention to? What do they see as the direction of the team? In short, what is important to them?

If they haven't told you, how do you find out? Occam's Razor tells us the simple way is the best. Ask them. Sometimes people (not just managers) seem to believe that others will intuitively understand what they want and so there is no need to say it. That's just human nature. The truth is, everyone is bad at reading people's minds – even if we genuinely care about that person, the relationship or what we are trying to accomplish. This is a great discussion topic for your first one-on-one meeting when you have a new manager.

You help your manager most by doing these things:

- Understand what is important to them.
- Align your work and goals to those things.
- Set up a regular, recurring one-on-one meeting series. More on this in the *Effective one-on-ones* with your managers and leaders section later.
- Seek clarification when you are asked to work on something that doesn't seem to align.
- Feed your manager the information they need in the way that works for them. Don't make them come looking for you when they need to know something. You should already have told them.
- Embrace a "no surprises" philosophy, especially for bad news. Everybody has a manager. If something bad happens, you have to consider that somewhere up in the org chart, questions are going to start flowing down and they are coming to your manager. The better you

can prepare them about whatever happened and what is being done about it, the better. If you can tell your manager, "The service is down for all users in Western Europe. We're still investigating. There doesn't seem to be any data loss. We'll have an update on progress in 30 minutes" it will be *incredibly* valuable. That lets them start communicating this up the chain maybe even before anyone else knows about it.

What about bad managers?

I would be painting a false picture if I didn't add to all of this something that you probably already know. There are *a lot* of bad managers out there. There are people who will see you as a cog in their machine, no matter how much you try to help them. There are people who will happily throw you under the bus to help themselves. There are people who will look you right in the face and lie as if it were their native language. And, as we've already discussed, there are people who really never wanted to be managers in the first place or who were never really taught how to be good at management.
None of that is good for you.
Nothing you do can fix people like that. In those cases, your best move may be to start looking for another role in the company with a better manager. John Maxwell says in his book *Leadership Gold* that people leave companies not because they dislike the company or their job, but to escape a bad manager. The good news is you don't really need to leave the whole company that you otherwise like. One of the advantages of a large organization is there are other roles and other managers. When you consider other roles, remember that you are interviewing that manager for the job of being your manager, just like they are interviewing you. The ultimate payback is that as a manager develops a reputation for not being able to keep a team together and losing talent, usually that will reflect on them.

But, and I need to stress this, even if you have a terrible manager and are working on making a move, for your own career safety, as long as you are still on the team, you can't just start ignoring the manager. Neither should you make negative comments about them to other team members. You should still do your best to apply the tips in this section. In addition, you should carefully document your accomplishments and make notes of your one-on-one discussions with your manager. Hang on to email exchanges and just file them away. This probably seems paranoid and, in fact, you probably won't end up needing any of this, but when you are in a bad situation, better safe than sorry.

Things your manager won't tell you

This section isn't really going to help you feel better. I wanted to include it just to set your expectations and let you know you aren't alone if you aren't getting clear answers to certain questions from your manager.

There are some things that, as employees, we really want and need to know. Arguably, that we *deserve* to know. Unfortunately, almost without exception, your manager in a large company is just not going to be able to tell you.

- Will I be promoted in the coming cycle?
- What specifically do I need to do to be promoted?
- If I do x, y and z, will I get the Lead position?
- What kind of pay raise can I expect this year?
- I'm about to buy a house, am I at risk for layoffs?

These are all perfectly reasonable questions. And you aren't going to get full and complete answers for any of them.

If you press them on it, most managers will try to fill in the gaps with non-committal answers. "You are doing a great job!" "Things are looking positive this year." "I hear great feedback about you." All nice words, but definitely nothing you can make plans around.

The better managers will simply tell you how these things are decided in the company and why they can't tell you for sure, but tell you what you need to do and what they can commit to doing for you in return. Sadly, this seems to be quite rare.

The simple fact is, that in almost any organization of size, your manager doesn't control who gets promoted. They can submit people; advocate for them; provide guidance to improve your chances, but they can almost never say, "You ship this release by the end of the quarter and you will get that promotion," which is really the binary clarity we would wish for.

The same is true with pay, bonuses and equity compensation. There is generally a budget, and there is a financial model for compensation changes. The model gives recommendations to a manager (who may be the manager of your manager or even higher). These are strongly influenced by your place in the pay band, as described in *Principle #2: Make a* map. Your quintile in your current pay band, most likely the smaller percentage any raise will be. Unfortunately, probably the first you will hear from your manager about where you are in the band is when you being near the top of it is used as an excuse for a very small increase. At whatever level the budget responsibility falls, that manager usually has some small latitude to adjust up or down.

Effective one-on-ones with your managers and leaders
A key part of establishing a strong and productive working relationship with your manager is to set up regular recurring one-on-one meetings (sometimes referred to as "1:1s"). You should work with your manager on the frequency and length of these meetings. Personally, I prefer 30 minutes once a week with my direct reports and every other week or monthly with indirect reports, but every manager has their own pattern. It is not uncommon that you may have longer or more frequent meetings when you are onboarding to a new team before settling into a long-term rhythm.

Once it is on the calendar, what will you talk about? After all, even a 30-minute meeting between any two software professionals costs about $100 or more just for the time spent (ignoring opportunity cost, infrastructure and all those other things that add up). You should think about how you are investing that time. Many managers will simply default to talking about project status – almost like a daily standup meeting. This is usually not a good way to spend that time. Managers do need to know status of things, but there are better ways to collect and share that information. If this keeps coming up as a topic, you might take the bull by the horns and ask if there is a better way you could be providing status updates so you don't have to cover it in your one-on-one time. Note how that turns it from "hey manager you are doing this wrong" to you saying "I feel like maybe I'm not making sure you have the information you need when you need it, without waiting for our meetings." It makes it a "you" thing, not a "them" thing. Even so, it is inevitable that some status topics will come up. It's not that we are banned from talking about task status; we just don't want to fall back on that rather than more substantial topics.

If we aren't talking about status, then what are we talking about? I'd suggest that *you* bring the agenda to the meeting. If your manager doesn't suggest doing this, you should bring it up. "Do you mind if I bring topics for our discussion each week." You may even want to send them the day before the meeting. And if you honestly don't have anything useful to talk about between the two of you, or you are scrambling to meet a tight deadline or whatever, it's 100% OK to just cancel that session. Try not to make a habit of canceling, but don't waste time when there's nothing to discuss.

Things to talk about with your manager:
- Feedback on your work.
- Questions about practices or workflows and perhaps suggestions on how they could be improved – and what part you could play in those improvements.
- What you see as your ranked list of priorities right now. And ask your manager to share their own list.
- Occasionally, ask your manager what their main concern or worry is right now. What keeps them up at night?
- Ask "What do you most need from me right now?"
- Discuss your career roadmap. What comes next? Where do you see yourself on that path? Where does your manager see you?
- Don't shy away from rapport building. Yes, I said don't waste the time on idle chit chat, but it is great to allow these meetings to get a little personal. Open up about interests and life challenges outside work. This is valuable to building that relationship of trust.

One thing you definitely should **not** do, or at least need to consider very carefully before doing, is complain about specific co-workers to your manager. Except in the most egregious cases, (in which really you should probably be talking to HR instead) this just doesn't work well. Most of the time it will just make you look bad. In some cases, you might say something like "I've noticed that sometimes I seem to be excluded from design discussions about *XYZ*. I feel like I have a contribution to make there. Do you have any guidance on how I can position myself better to be part of those decisions?" You may notice a pattern here. Even if the problem is 100% on the other person, you are talking about it in terms of what *you* can change. It may seem silly, but it does genuinely play better when a manager hears it phrased this way.

I'd strongly encourage that you take careful notes during your meetings. If you know your agenda topics in advance, you can prepare your notes by already having those written. If there are some you don't get to, you can move them to next time or just cross them out or whatever suits your style. Include your current priority list in the notes.

You don't need a full transcript of the meeting, but capture the key points and especially any follow up items for either of you. Many people like to use a single document with the whole history of their 1:1 notes (most recent at the top works best). Just keep these notes for yourself.

You'll be better prepared for the next 1:1 meeting. You won't forget to follow up on things you said you would do. You can remember actions your manager said they would do.

I'd also encourage you to send a separate summarized and "sanitized" version of these notes to your manager, in email or whatever you two agree works best. It gives a chance to catch things like "Oh no, that's not what I meant." Things like this really tend to set you apart from your peers.

You'll find that this set of notes become useful during review time and when updating your résumé in the future.

Meetings

We all hate them. We all believe we're spending too much time in them – and we're probably right about that. However, getting people together to make plans and sort through problems is just a necessity. We hate them because they are so often badly done.

Here are some tips to make meetings work better and be more productive, so we can be back to the other parts of our jobs.

Basic meeting etiquette

Experience has taught me that a lot of people, no matter their role, struggle with this. The explosion of remote work and video meetings has actually made this worse. It seems worth capturing a few basics of meeting etiquette. As you read this short set of points, you'll see they are really all related to respect. Being an effective and engaged participant shows respect not only to the organizer and the other attendees, but really to the overall process of trying to make the right things happen.

Spoiler Alert: one key point here is if you can't be an effective and engaged participant in the meeting because you have something else more important to do, you don't care enough about the topic, or whatever, it's almost always better just to decline the meeting.

- **Come prepared.** Hopefully, you know why someone is inviting you to a meeting. The invitation should have an agenda or at least be clear about what is being discussed and the desired end result. If it doesn't you should ask the person who invited you. It's very difficult to come prepared if you don't know what it is about.

  If there are documents or other materials provided, read them. If the meeting is code related, review the code in question in advance so you can come with an opinion.

  This is not a criticism, but if you aren't willing to do this level of preparation, you probably aren't going to be a useful voice in this meeting and should just consider declining.

- **Don't multitask.** A good friend has a mantra that if you feel you can multitask in a meeting, you really shouldn't be there. That sounds brutal, but there is a lot of wisdom in it.

  If you have something genuinely more important to do, don't come. Don't be the person sitting at the conference table furiously banging away on the keyboard trying to get a server back up. Just excuse yourself and go do the urgent thing.

  We've all seen the situation, particularly on video meetings, where at some point, someone gets called on by name to give an opinion and they've been doing something else and have to ask for the question to be repeated so they can give an off the cuff answer. Most of us have done it, and yet when we see it, we feel embarrassed for that person being caught out.

  We all like to think we can multitask. Maybe we even call it out as a personal virtue, but the cold science fact is that people can't multitask. We can't do multiple high-level brain tasks at one time. Yes, we can walk and chew gum, we can breathe and pump blood while we write a book, but we can't really listen and participate in a meeting while we write code, catch up on our email or play a game of Solitaire.

- **Actually listen.** This sounds silly. Of course we're listening, right? Well….probably not. Most people spend most of the time they aren't talking thinking of what they are going to say the next time they speak, and so, because we can't really multitask, we aren't listening at all.

  In the action steps for *Principle #5: Don't be annoying*, I mentioned looking for opportunities for active listening. There are many benefits to active listening, but I want to mention two in the context of meeting etiquette. One is that the other person hears in your reflecting back to them that you were actually listening to them, which shows you value their communication even if you don't agree. The other is that it is *impossible* to use active listening if you aren't actually listening. It forces you to do the right thing.

You might even jot a few quick notes while they are talking to organize what they have said and what you want to say about it.

- **Restating and building on.** Extending basic active listening is to adopt an approach of "restating" what the person has said. Such as, "If I can just restate what you said to make sure I'm clear, you are saying it doesn't matter if we have redundancy at the database level because it is very unlikely we'll ever have an outage. Is that right?"

  This gives you a chance to say what you think you heard and the other person to correct what you have misunderstood or they misstated.

  "Building" or "building on" is a bit related. It allows us to take another idea that has been raised and extend on it or change it without just ignoring it or casting it aside. "Just building on what Joe said, from my own testing I know that moving to .Net Core will give us substantial performance improvements. I've actually done some preliminary benchmarks on our part of the code that I can share."

  Building is a bit like saying "I agree and…" or "I agree but…"

  Both of these techniques can be very useful.

- **Don't interrupt people.** The stereotypical engineer tends to be opinionated and maybe a bit on the loud and expressive side, but that's not all of us. Our personality includes elements of our culture, family, gender and other factors; as well as just the way we are. People interrupting one another or just talking over them is something we see all too often. *One thing we still see a lot and that is engineers using big booming voices to talk over engineers who are more reserved or with quieter voices.* **Let's just stop doing that.**

The basics of running a meeting

The point of this section isn't to turn you into a meeting scheduler and note taker. To get things we want, even engineering design decisions, we need communication – and meetings are one way that communication happens. This is about enabling you to get things you need so you can make progress.

Don't rely on *someone else* to set up and run meetings that you need to have. In some teams, you will have a Technical Program Manager (TPM) or a Project Manager or someone else who seems to drive a lot of the meetings. They can be a helpful resource, but it usually isn't their job to run your meetings for you.
Generally speaking, even if there is someone who seems to run meetings as a big part of their job, they won't like it if you assume they are there to handle yours. You should coordinate with them in advance though, just to understand how involved they would like to be.

If there is an existing meeting that has the right people in it for something you want to discuss, talk to the owner of that meeting *in advance* about taking some amount of time for your topic. If it is a recurring meeting, there will hopefully be an agenda and a beforehand the meeting owner will often ask the attendees if there are items to add to the agenda. Or at the end of one session there might be discussion about the agenda for the next meeting. If that works for your topic, that's a good way to go.

Before the meeting

When you've determined that you need to set up a meeting yourself, figure out who needs to be there and who should be included as optional attendees. You want to include the set of people you must have to reach the outcome you want from the meeting – a decision, enough review sign-off to proceed with a design, etc. You may want to ask those people if there are others who *must* be part of the discussion. In general, though, the smaller the meeting the more likely you are to come to a result.

In *Principle #1: Nail your job*, I talked about knowing your tools, including the calendar system your team uses. You are about to make use of those skills to set up your meeting by following these steps:

- Give the meeting a clear and meaningful subject, such as "Review database redundancy design."
- Select a meeting length that allows you to actually get to the end point you desire. Not many substantial topics can be resolved in 30 minutes. If you need more than an hour, particularly if you have more than two or three other participants, consider breaking up the meeting into multiple meetings, each with its own goal. It will just be easier to fit it on people's calendars. *Note:* there is a trend to not starting meetings directly on the hour or half hour, but like 5 minutes after. The idea here is to let people who were in one meeting right before this one to take care of any quick tasks they need to in between. This is another area where you just have to pay attention to what is normal where you work.
- Include the required and optional attendees.
- Once you have the length and required attendees, look at their calendars to find a place they are available. If there are one or two people with conflicts, you might reach out to them and ask if they can free up that time that works for everyone else. That may or may not be possible, but worth asking.

- If this will include online participants, include the link to the meeting. This is frequently forgotten and causes a last-minute scramble of people trying to join a meeting and having no link.
- OK, this is important. In the text of the invitation include a sentence or two about the meeting and the end goal. It's good to include an agenda for the discussion, especially if multiple people have parts to play in the meeting. People *hate* getting meeting invites without this information and will often just reject the meeting if it isn't there. If something is important enough to take people into a meeting, it is important enough for you to write a few words about it in advance.
- Links to documents to be discussed or pre-reading. If you expect people to come to the meeting having already read it, make sure you are clear about that. Otherwise, plan on doing it the "Amazon way" and spending the first part of the meeting with everyone reading. I actually prefer this approach, but you'll have to decide what normal looks like in your organization.

Before the meeting happens, pay attention to who has accepted and declined the meeting. If a key person declines, you may need to consider moving the meeting so they can attend.

During the meeting
It is very difficult to drive a meeting discussion *and* take notes as it is happening.
Depending on the situation, recording the meeting can be very helpful. Online tools make this an easy process and the way we got used to working in the COVID-19 pandemic made recordings much more accepted. You might also consider recording even just the audio during a meeting so you ensure

your notes are complete later. You'll want to comply with legal and policy requirements around doing that in your company. Some note taking tools, like Microsoft OneNote™, have interesting tools to combine audio recordings with typed notes, keeping the two in sync.

If you are the one driving the meeting or especially if you are projecting to demonstrate something or present information, it can be difficult to also take notes. You might ask another attendee in advance if they would take the notes.

Whatever tools you use and whomever takes the notes, you don't need a transcript of the entire meeting but you very much need these things:

- Important points raised and who raised them
- Key decisions
- Blocking issues
- Action items for follow-up, including who will own them and what date you can expect them to deal with it.

As you move through the discussion, if there is someone who seems to be sitting quietly or holding back, invite them to share their thoughts. If they decline, that's fine, but don't let just a small number of people dominate the conversation.

Keep an eye on the clock. It's better to close the meeting on time and schedule another follow-up meeting than to run over time. Although, if it is a hard crowd to get together, you might actually ask what they prefer when it becomes clear you will all need more time.

It is a good idea at the end of the meeting to review this while you have everyone together. They can help fill in any gaps or correct anything you got wrong.

After the meeting

Collect the notes and results of the meeting and send them to all the people who were invited – even if they didn't attend. Depending on how you do things, you might want to store them in a shared document folder or other repository for future reference. You've invested a lot in planning and having the meeting. Don't stop there. Capture the results. Otherwise, you will probably find yourself discussing the same thing in the future because everyone forgets the conclusion.

Did you get to the result you needed? If not, you may be scheduling a follow-up meeting. If there were particular people who were opposed or just not fully aligned with the goal, you should talk with them separately and understand their point of view. This will help the next meeting be more successful.

Brown bag sessions

Encourage the team to set up information sharing sessions. Often these are called "brown bag sessions" or "lunch and learn meetings" because they are often held over lunch time and people bring their lunch with them to the discussion. You can have them at any time of day though and they work well over video conferencing as well as in person.

A team who is just starting on this might decide to have one session a month, let's say on the first Thursday in the afternoon. Just whenever works for the team.

Broad participation should be encouraged, especially for lower leveled team members. The person driving the discussion is not really "teaching" or "presenting" so much as they are facilitating a discussion.

For example, maybe a team member is really passionate about some new cloud technology. They might gather a little information about it, possibly gather up some links about it, maybe some sample code if that is appropriate. They kick off the discussion by introducing the topic and why they are interested in it. They can tell what they have learned, maybe show a little demo, maybe a YouTube video about, or whatever seems to fit. All along the way, team members can speak up. Maybe they have experiences with it too. Maybe they read something about it. Maybe they know some problems with it that aren't immediately apparent.

The person facilitating doesn't need to be an expert. They don't need to be trying to pitch the team to use it for a particular part of a current project. It's just a discussion between engineering peers.

In fact, if you want to try this out, just pick out a topic you care about and schedule the time to discuss it. The goal is to keep the level of preparation friction to a minimum. You aren't teaching a class; you are all just eating your lunch together and talking about tech stuff.

If the meeting is slated for 45 minutes and this topic only goes on for 25 minutes, that's OK. People can break up early, or talk about other topics.

If the team members are comfortable recording these sessions and posting them on some shared drive, then bonus points for that, but it isn't required. It is a good idea to capture at least a few notes about it and post those just so people who weren't there can get some idea and follow up with questions.

These sessions promote team communication and morale and they inspire people to "connect the dots" by providing more "dots" for them to connect at some future time.

Another benefit is that they become tools for people on the team (like *you*) to establish their expertise and begin to broaden their circle of impact and influence. This is one way the next set of influencers in an organization will begin to emerge.

Providing feedback

The internet has made us all professional reviewers.

> "5 stars! Would totally eat these tacos again!!!"
>
> "1 star! Can I give it zero stars? This movie was so bad even the popcorn didn't make it better!"

As we do our work, most often we are working with others. This leads to opportunities to provide our "review" of their performance. How can we do that effectively?

Be liberal with meaningful public compliments and praise

Be the kind of person who is free in giving compliments. It costs you nothing to point out, in front of other team members (and that part is important), that someone did a great job on something – even if they really did a "good" job rather than a great one. Look for opportunities to do this, even if you are the only one doing it at first. Most likely, it will catch on and other people on the team will start doing it. No matter your title or position or how long you've been with the team, this is a clear chance to be influential in the spirit of the team and how they work together.

A few examples of where you can do this:

- In your daily standup meeting. "Just a quick shout out to Jim for helping me get the data adapter working yesterday. I learned a lot and was able to complete my task. I really appreciate it."
- In your team messaging channel. Many teams have a Kudos or Shout Outs thread for this. Even if you don't just tack it on the end of a status update. "We just released to production! Couldn't have done it without the extra time Angela and Henry put in on the last minute Terraform problem after we moved to the new framework."

- In a retrospective meeting. Formats vary but usually these meetings cover what went well, what needs improvement, and lessons learned. This is a great place to give some praise.
- When the person you are praising isn't in the room, it can actually be even more meaningful to those hearing.

Note that all of these examples are clear about what is being praised and they are all about *real and impactful* things. Saying "Bob is great," is not really meaningful to Bob or anyone else, and it also takes away the learning opportunity for the rest of the team about what is noteworthy.

Keep doing this even if other people aren't jumping in. And do it even if no one gives you praise. It will all come around eventually.
A last note about this. We're talking about publicly *praising* people. If someone messed up, they need that feedback too, but don't just swap in critiques for praise in those examples I listed. Give that feedback in private conversations. Remember the old adage to praise in public and criticize in private.

Just say "no" to the compliment sandwich

Regarding giving criticism or negative feedback, I want to touch on an old idea of the so-called "compliment sandwich" (also known as the praise or criticism sandwich, among other names).

The exact origin is unclear but this has "management consultant" written all over it. It dates back to at least the mid-1940s but had renewed popularity after being featured in the 1984 book *Mary Kay on People Management* by Mary Kay Ash. The idea of that is to start by giving a compliment, then give a criticism, and then end with another compliment.

Honestly, it's just a terrible, counter-productive practice. The formula is transparent, which people tend not to like – especially the hard-edged folks in the software business. More importantly, the point of the communication is to deliver the negative feedback in the middle, but most people will, essentially, hear two-thirds of the message as good things about them and not hear that part in the middle…which was the whole point. The message you intend to communicate (albeit in a nice, soft way) is not what the receiver will actually receive.

It is really a poor way to communicate, period. And it's not just my opinion, there is a lot of research backing up the ineffectiveness of this technique. Check out the links to the articles by Roger Schwarz (*Harvard Business Review*) and Steve Lowisz (*Forbes*) in the *Reading List* section, or just do a quick web search about it.

In her book *Dare to Lead*, Brené Brown repeats a slogan from a 12-step Alcoholics Anonymous meeting "Clear is kind. Unclear is unkind." If you need to offer genuine, accurate negative feedback to someone, the kindest way to do that is with clarity. Saying a string of things that reduces that clarity is not kind. It can be confusing to the listener and ultimately frustrating to you. The sandwich *seems* like it would be kind, but it isn't. This may seem counter-intuitive, but it's just how it works out.

Give genuine feedback

Most companies use some formal system of peer feedback for purposes of evaluation cycles or promotion decisions. Sometimes this is referred to as "360 (as in degrees) feedback." In other situations, a co-worker or a co-worker's manager might reach out to you directly and solicit feedback either on their general performance or their work on a particular task or project. And there may be cases where you just feel you need to provide some feedback proactively and reach out either to the person or their manager.

How can you best provide these kinds of commentary in a useful and productive way?

First, let's acknowledge that this can be a delicate matter. If someone is doing great work and you just want to praise them, that's easy (and we've already covered that). It becomes more difficult when you need to deliver a less positive message. Even when things have not gone as well as they might have, or that we wish they had, the goal here is improvement, not finger pointing and blame. If the person receiving your feedback views your words as an attack, they are not going to benefit from what you are trying to communicate. Note that last sentence is about how the receiver *hears* the message, not what you actually said. It's true that there is definitely a limit to how we can message something to make sure the other person takes it as we intend. That doesn't absolve us of trying to keep the message accurate but still try to make it heard, so it can be useful. The only rule of thumb we really have here is how *we* would perceive that message if someone gave it to us. Even then, not everyone is the same, so there is no guarantee. All we can do is try, but without losing the actual feedback.

Here are a few guidelines to help you craft feedback.

Be honest. Let's just agree you aren't intending to use fake or exaggerated feedback to torpedo people (you wouldn't be the first, but that's not a productive career approach long term). Even so, you need to really walk through the feedback you are going to give and make sure it is objective and accurate.

- **Be brief, clear and direct.** This can be the most difficult part, especially the directness. When people are developing the skill of giving feedback, they tend to feel that they need to give exhaustive history with example after example, as if it were evidence in a criminal trial. This often happens when you are reacting to something that impacted you immediately after it happened and, frankly, you are just angry about it. Or they may get caught up in trying to soften the message to protect the feelings of the other person. In either case, you end up with so many words that the real message is lost. The best feedback is detailed enough to cover the situation but short enough to be clear and readable. Don't get carried away. When in doubt, you might ask a trusted friend or perhaps a significant other to review it and give you their thoughts on the writing. Be professional. Focus on the behavior and result, not the person or your feelings.
- **Use examples.** In the section *Dealing with Human Resources*, I refer to the Situation-Behavior-Impact model. That's a great way to capture examples in a way that is clear and direct and focuses just on the facts. If there are many examples, just give, perhaps, two of them and then say you can share additional examples.
- **Offer support and invite a conversation.** These things help cast the feedback you are offering in a positive light. If you are providing direct feedback to a person, it's not out of place to offer them support in dealing with the feedback or any gaps in experience or understanding they may have. Again, you need to do this delicately so it doesn't end up sounding like they are terrible and you are amazing and they need your help to improve. If you doubt that you can come up

with words that fit the situation, just leave this out, but if you can find a way to offer your assistance, it can really smooth the message – even something like offering an example of something helpful they bring to the team. One thing you should definitely do is offer a follow up conversation about the feedback.

- **Let it sit overnight.** When you write up feedback either to send by email or some electronic means, or if you are just organizing your thoughts before an in-person conversation, let it sit overnight and then read it with fresh eyes. Especially if this is something that has come up in the heat of the moment, this delay brings fresh perspective. This also means that, if there is a due date on this feedback, you can't procrastinate until the last minute. Leave some time to let it sit.

Many organizations, particularly those with a strong culture of giving feedback, offer training around giving feedback and often that involves some practice in giving and receiving it. If your company does that, take advantage of it. One final note of caution, though. As you develop a reputation for giving thoughtful, effective feedback, you may find yourself deluged with people including you in their list for peer feedback (if your workplace uses such a system). Generally speaking, you aren't obligated to respond to all of those feedback requests. I've spoken to developers for whom this became a significant burden. It's usually OK to be selective about which ones you answer.

When things go wrong

You made a mistake. Now what?

In work and in life, there are *many* types of mistakes. Luckily, as far as the software engineering workplace is concerned, there are really just a couple categories that apply. There are mistakes involving people and there are mistakes involving technology.

There's a common thread with handling either kind of mistake and that is to take responsibility for it. Don't try to rationalize it and clearly and openly communicate what happened. This sounds like just a tactic, but really this is just the right thing to do. The disarming power of simply standing up and taking responsibility will probably surprise you. It's a powerful first step in correcting whatever happened and minimizing the lasting impact on your career.

Mistakes involving people and relationships

Let's talk about the people ones first. We're working hard and there is often a fair amount of pressure. Those common situations can lead to discussions that can grow heated at times. Then someone says something insensitive or rude. This leads to hurt feelings and a breakdown in those relationships.

Depending on the nature of the comment or action, it can rise to the level that HR needs to become involved, and really that is no fun. In most cases, people get mad, sad or discouraged. They may feel isolated. All of those things impact their productivity and can have lasting impacts on team cohesion and progress.

If you have made this kind of mistake, I encourage you to quickly do two things. Apologize to the person and take responsibility for it. If you recognize the problem right after the remark was made, in a meeting for example, apologize right there and in front of everyone. Don't try to justify or excuse it, simply apologize. If you realize the mistake after the meeting has already ended, apologize directly to the person. Don't use text or email or online messaging. Either call them on the phone or do a video call or see them in person. Then follow up with whomever else heard it happen as a group – email or messaging is fine for this – and apologize to the injured party and all the attendees together, so they all see you doing it. This is hard, but it is very important.

Don't automatically assume everything is fine once you've apologized. You are really going to have to watch and respond to the cues from the other person. Sometimes, it will just be water under the bridge. In other cases, you'll have some rebuilding to do to restore the level of trust in that relationship.

There's another flavor to people mistakes and that is excluding or discounting someone from involvement in something when they should have been involved, or, at least, they feel like they should have been involved. In this case, you should have a conversation with them directly. You usually don't need to apologize to the whole team or group or other meeting attendees. This might start with something like, "I've heard you were upset I didn't pull you into the new API design meeting. I definitely didn't mean to exclude you. My intention was just to keep the discussion small until we were farther along and let everyone else just focus on their work. Now that I know your feelings, I'll include you in these discussions going forward."

Mistakes involving technology

According to Albert Einstein, if you have made a mistake, first let me say "congratulations." You tried something new. (I'll caveat that to say that if the thing you tried was to release to production before testing, that's not really a new idea. Don't do that.)

> "Anyone who has never made a mistake has never tried anything new."
>
> Albert Einstein

Again, the first step when you know you made a mistake is to raise your hand and call attention to it. Don't be the person who decides to just wait until someone tracks you down from check ins or logs.

Depending on the impact of the mistake, there is going to be some level of discussion about this. Sometimes it is called a post-mortem, root cause analysis, debrief, lessons learned or five whys. In a healthy environment, the purpose of these should be to figure out how the bad thing was allowed to happen and how to prevent it from happening in the future. These could include both technical steps as well as workflow or process steps.

I'm a big fan of the "Five Whys" process, which, like many things agile and lean, originated at Toyota Motor Corporation. See https://tulip.co/glossary/five-whys/ for more information.

> **Example of a Five Whys session**
> **Q:** Why did the service go offline?
> **A:** Bill made a code change that introduced a bug in accessing the user profile database.
> **Q:** Why didn't the unit test find that bug?
> **A:** The data access in the Test system is different from

> Production. It worked in Test.
>
> **Q:** Why is the Test system different?
> **A:** 3 months ago, we changed the data configuration on Production for better scaling. Test didn't need to scale, so it just didn't seem important.
>
> **Q:** Why wasn't the problem found in code review?
> **A:** The code was reviewed and approved by two other engineers, but neither of them were familiar with this Prod scaling change in this particular area of the code. So really, we had the wrong reviewers on this PR.
>
> … and so on.

Now, I've been around long enough to know it is not always going to be so calm, methodical and expletive free as this. When people are in the middle of going berserk due to an outage and are mad at you because you made the mistake, the best thing you can to after taking responsibility is to keep refocusing on "let's get the system restored by pushing a new change (or rolling back or whatever) and then we can get to the bottom on how exactly it happened." Try to be the calm voice of reason, even though it is, for lack of a better term, your fault. Getting things back online for customers must be the full focus.

I'll add one more thing here because I know you are thinking about it.
If the place you work in is the kind of place that would terminate an employee over this kind of mistake (unless it is a pattern or an engineer who bypassed policy or something like that), really that's not the kind of place you want to work anyway. You want to skip ahead to the section titled *The breaking point*.

If the mistake we are talking about here is that you advocated a design or a tool usage that ended up not meeting the need,

OK. Still take responsibility for that. Assuming you made the best decision you could make at the time with the information that was available, that's the best you can do. Engineering is always about making tradeoffs with imperfect data. We just strive to do our best. This is really the kind of mistake that Einstein quote refers to. In almost any organization worth being part of, a person will do better if they make decisions, even if they are not always right, and moves ahead to the *next* decision and keeps going. Correcting along the way with the best decision we can take with the situation as it is at the time. Bill Hammack describes this as "the engineering method" in his book *The Things We Make*. His book isn't about software engineering, but the concepts still apply in our world.

Dealing with Human Resources (HR)

The most basic question is "what does Human Resources really even do?" It's a good question, especially because the name "Human Resources" is so broad and all encompassing.

HR functions include:

- **Talent Acquisition/Recruiting**
  Managing the job posting, interviewing and hiring process. It is fairly common for this process, or much of it, to be handled through a Recruiting team, separate from the core HR team in larger companies.

- **Employment law compliance**
  The legal picture for companies, especially if the operate across multiple US states and countries, can be very complex. This includes all kinds of requirements around reporting and regulations related to employees. In some companies, this is an organic part of the HR organization, in others it may fall under a Legal organization.

- **Compensation & Benefits**
  Salaries and hourly wages, time tracking, bonuses, healthcare, retirement plans, stock compensation and other benefits. Like recruiting, this is often split into a separate Payroll team in organizations of size, and may fall under a Finance team.

- **Employee Relations**
  Dealing with employee grievances and disputes. This is probably the main thing employees think of when they think of what HR does.
- **Performance Management**
  Employee performance review and management processes vary quite a bit across companies, but whatever the process, HR manages it. This also often includes defining the career ladders and job architectures covered in *Principle #2: Make a map* that help employees understand what their career path at the company looks like.
- **Training & Development**
  For employees, this is probably one of the least well utilized aspects of HR. Many organizations have a variety of training and professional education materials available including access to free third-party resources, in-house training, helpful articles and videos and even assistance in paying for outside training and certification.
- **HR Operations**
  This includes deploying and managing Human Resource Information Systems (HRIS) systems like Workday, PeopleSoft or in-house created tools. These provide access to org charts, time off tracking, employee data and history.
- **Diversity, Equity & Inclusion**
  All the efforts to ensure the workplace is a fair and inclusive place to work, ranging from education programs to regulatory compliance tracking.

Note that it is common that some (or even all) of these functions to be outsourced to external provider.

Throughout my career, I've always heard the message that employees should avoid talking to HR unless you really feel you have no other choice. As a manager, even though I have always met regularly with, and had a good relationship with my HR contact (often called an "HR Business Partner"), I've generally led people on my teams to avoid reaching out to them unless really needed.

I have come to believe I was wrong about that. We should break that common notion that talking to HR means you are "in trouble."

The HR professionals I interviewed consistently felt they were an under-utilized resource for employee career development. Some companies divide these responsibilities for career development in different ways, but you should know your HR contact. They can always at least help you find the correct person if it isn't them. One HR pro said, "Employees should view HR as a partner, not the police."

When you join a new team, you may want to do just a brief 15-minute introductory meeting with them, so if you need their help in the future, they already who you are.

If you feel you have been subjected to discrimination, retaliation, illegal conduct or if you feel you are not safe, then you should talk to HR. If your direct manager is not the person involved in that conduct, then you may want to talk to them first, but they will almost certainly direct you to HR. Once you raise an HR complaint about these serious matters involving other co-workers, you really can't put that genie back in the bottle. It will set off a series of events that can have repercussions on all the parties. I'm not saying you shouldn't do it. I'm saying you certainly shouldn't do it frivolously.

HR professionals have their own standards and requirements of confidentiality. In general, employees can expect a very high level of confidentiality unless the context of their issue involves criminal activity, assault, harassment or things of that nature. Unlike a lawyer, doctor or clergy, they are not always subject to broad requirements or expectations of confidentiality. However, HR works closely with Legal teams and can involve an in-house lawyer to establish attorney-client privilege around those discussions to protect those conversations.

In some circumstances, information you provide can be shared with your management chain – particularly if the situation is between you and another employee, unless the other person is that manager. The exact bounds of this can vary by location and company policies. When in doubt, it is wise to ask how it will be handled and who will know **before** you get into the details. If your complaint is about another person on the team and HR determines the need to speak to that person, you should expect they will not share your information with them. However, that person may still deduce from the context who made the complaint.

Remember, while the people in your HR team are usually helpful and friendly by nature, and they may often provide beneficial support to the employee, the primary role of HR is to safeguard the interests of the company, ensure it complies with all the complexities of employment laws and protect it from liability.

If you are going to escalate an issue to HR here are some things you should do to prepare:

- Write a brief statement, a few sentences in a paragraph, describing the issue. It may seem strange that I suggest you write this in advance. These conversations can become emotional, so it is just easier to do it before the actual discussion.
- Consider using the Situation-Behavior-Impact, or SBI, model. I'm going to deliberately use an incredibly bad scenario in this example that is clearly over anyone's line of propriety.
  Situation is what was going on. "I was in a design review meeting with Bob, Steve and Sally."

Behavior is what someone did in that situation. "Steve gave some harsh feedback about my work and then continued making comments relating my race to the quality of my work."

Impact is the result of that behavior in the situation. "I was already shocked by the harshness of the feedback but the race-related comments just knocked me off my feet. Bob and Sally were silent and looked shocked. Bob said we should end the meeting and we'd come back to it later. I went back to my desk and gathered my things and went home early. Since then, my productivity on the project has been significantly impacted.

- Note the timeline of events. This doesn't need to be super detailed, but you should organize your thoughts.
- Collect any direct supporting evidence. This may be emails, Slack messages, Basecamp comments, etc. Just anything captures the problem behavior. At this stage, *do not* reach out to other team members for supporting statements or encourage others to contact HR also. HR will provide direction and support for any of this if it is appropriate.
- Make copies of any materials you have and store them outside of company property. Even a locked desk drawer in your workspace is company property and you have no expectation of privacy there.

HR can't help with everything. It is common to have differences of opinion and clashing personalities with co-workers. Unless those differences cross those legal bounds of discrimination and safety, or violate internal policies, help from HR is likely going to be more in the form of a helpful conversation rather than direct intervention. Depending on the HR person involved or the organization, they may offer you some guidance or perhaps point you to some information to give you some tools to better deal with the situation, but it is unlikely they will intervene directly.

While it would be inappropriate to retaliate against an employee in any way for making an HR complaint, there is a human reality that if you become known as a person who is always running to HR for any perceived slight, however minor, that is going to become an issue for you. Don't do that!

If you are the subject of an HR complaint, this alone is not necessarily a problem. It is certainly possible that someone can raise a groundless or exaggerated complaint and the internal investigation will uncover that. However, you should also collect any evidence you have and store copies of it off of company property. When you are interviewed by HR, everything you say is "on the record" so you should think carefully about your responses. If you are being accused of something rising to criminal behavior, or if you have concerns you may not be treated fairly even in a non-criminal situation, you may want to contacting a lawyer specializing in employment matters.

If this section has made you nervous, just know that I've been in this business for decades and have had ZERO negative interaction with HR. There have been a couple of occasions when I've been asked questions as part of an investigation about another employee but even that is a tiny number of interactions. Most people behave professionally enough at work that it isn't a widespread problem. Thank goodness.

Going to HR with a serious complaint is a bit like calling the emergency number on your phone. They are there to help and support in important and delicate situations, but you don't hit that emergency dial button if your neighbor just didn't clean up after their dog.

The breaking point

Before you get so frustrated that either your performance suffers and endangers your future in the job you have, or you just get to the point you feel you are burned out and have no choice but to leave, pause for a moment.

Pay attention to your sleep habits. Are you working too late and then you are too keyed up to sleep properly? Does this end up with you getting a slow start the next day and getting into a repeating cycle? Pay attention to that and break that cycle. You aren't going to make real progress on your work when you are in that state. Make it a point to stop working and thinking about work earlier in the evening. Wind down. Do something mindless and non-work related like watch a movie that makes you laugh, play a video game, read (something that isn't job related). And get a good night's sleep. It will pay dividends in reduced stress and sharper focus.

Recharge away from work. When was the last time you took a day off and truly disconnected? How about three or four days? The disconnecting part is important. Yes, it is a sad fact that our reward for taking a day off is that we come back to all the work we missed, which isn't great. But you need that time off to disconnect. It's really taking the encouragement to get a good night's sleep one step further. Spend time with your friends, your family, your dog, or just yourself. Whatever means "relaxation" for you.

Find someone you can help. Sounds trite, I know, but if you change the focus from yourself to serving someone else, it will help you refocus your own mental energy. This isn't necessarily building houses in Honduras or spending your weekends working in a food bank (although I've known many people who have found those things very rewarding). It can be as simple as spending time with another co-worker who is struggling with some technical concept two desks away from yours, maybe on another project.

Learn to be OK with imperfection and ambiguity. One of the biggest stumbling blocks many of us have in this profession is being hooked on perfection or knowing all the details. It's a powerful attraction and it's very hard to stop. One step at a time, just learn to let things go – not the truly important things, but not everything is equally important or equally your responsibility. If you are a person who second-guesses other people's work, goes back and reviews their check-ins after they've already been reviewed and approved by the right people, you have to learn to be content letting them try and sometimes fail on their own. If you feel like you need to constantly probe all the design documents to look for "plot holes" or risks that aren't called out, even when it isn't your area of ownership, stop looking. Focus on your area unless someone asks for your help and review. Just loosen your grip a little bit. Realistically, it is unlikely that you and you alone are holding everything together, even if it sometimes feels like you are. You can't carry all that weight yourself.

> **A few words about ambiguity and uncertainty**
> Accepting a degree of uncertainty is really core to engineering and it's one of the key things that separates science, which really is a pursuit of certainty, from engineering, which is a pragmatic search for "good enough" and "suitability to purpose" within the constraints at hand.
> I've often told recent computer science grads that not many places actually do "computer science." We do "software engineering" and those are quite different things.
> This doesn't mean you should throw caution to the wind and just do whatever. But if you keep this perspective in mind and continue to push forward making the best decisions you can reasonably make with the time, people and other constraints you face, you'll do OK more often than not. When you don't do OK you pause, figure out what went wrong and how you could have better seen that ahead of time, and then move forward again with the lesson learned. You'll get farther, faster with this approach than indulging in analysis paralysis and moving so slowly that you miss the moment.

When an ending becomes necessary
Author Dr. Henry Cloud wrote a book called *Necessary Endings* about learning when to let go of things that aren't working. Sometimes, that can include a job, even if it pays well and your boss thinks you're awesome. That doesn't mean it is right for you to continue at this moment in your life. And at other times, it isn't our choice to move on. Unfortunately, layoffs and terminations are real things that happen.

Let's fast forward. Let's say you have been patient. You've learned and applied the principles I've outlined and you've tried to learn from other influential people in the organization – and it is just not working.

Now what?

There are times when the organization, or some of the people in it, just leave you no real option than to take your skills and move on. That doesn't mean you've wasted your time at the company you are at. Maybe it's not a great fit for you. Maybe you've outgrown it or learned what you feel you can learn there. Knowing when to move on is a strength, not a weakness.

The process of changing jobs is probably not one you look forward to. It involves a taxing process of searching, interviewing, negotiating an offer and then of coming up to speed with a new team and, possibly, a whole new type of business.

Often, the tenacious mindset of the software engineer works against their own interests and they either become accepting of the inertia of the situation, because the effort needed to make a change seems distasteful, or they feel the need to "finish the job" or "fix the problem." Ultimately, each person has to make the decision for themselves about if and when to make a career change.

Keep in mind a couple things though. First, generally speaking, this should definitely be a step up. Be careful of the inclination to "run **away**" from a bad situation – unless it is genuinely toxic or dangerous. Changes should see you "running **to**" something good. An opportunity to grow your responsibility and ownership – and generally to increase your compensation. Second, you spend a lot of your waking hours at work. Hopefully, it's not the dominating characteristic of your life, but it's a big part. It should be an overall positive experience, not something that you dread when the alarm clock goes off every morning.

When the time comes, don't feel like you are stuck. Take what you've learned and go on to your next adventure. And apply these same principles in that great new role! Starting again with Principle #1, and nail those basics.

Ultimatums

Sometimes we feel unappreciated, under-rewarded or just get mad at our job or our leadership. When this happens, it can be tempting to give an ultimatum. "Give me a 10% raise or I'm taking another position."

It is *incredibly* rare that this strategy works. Most large companies in particular just have a "no ultimatums" policy – either unwritten or sometimes actually written. If you are really ready to walk out the door and have other options in hand, you really should just do it. Often, in cases where an employee demands a pay bump to stay and receives it, they are gone within a short time anyway. Mentally, they have one foot out the door already when they make the demand.

It is possible to have a conversation with your manager about compensation *without* an ultimatum. You can show data for other similar roles in the area, for example. You can talk about your performance metrics and positive feedback you've received. Once you stray into something that looks like an ultimatum, the spirit of that conversation just changes and it feels like a threat. People just don't like threats (no surprise) and they don't want to be seen as someone who responds to threats.

Exit interviews

It's much less common these days, but some companies still like to do "exit interviews." I've always found this puzzling. You've either already voted with your feet and are leaving by choice, or you have been let go and are already mad about that. Usually, there's no mystery by that time. You've probably had discussions with your management about it, perhaps several times. What can come of these exit interviews? You don't like the company direction. You didn't like the compensation. You thought the CEO was dumb. Whatever it is, your exit interview is really not going to change those things. The most likely result is you will be perhaps *too forthcoming* in the exit interview and risk burning the bridge to possibly return to that company in another role in the future. There's just no good that can come of it.

If you are confronted with a request for an exit interview, just don't. Even in the few places that do them, they are often optional. If someone schedules one for you, decline it or ignore it.

When it's not your choice - layoffs and job loss

Given the realities of where we are as I write this in the tech employment cycle, jobs come and go. That's just the unfortunate truth. Often, it isn't even because you did something wrong – that's one of the things that makes it more difficult. By the time you are informed that you are being laid off, there is usually nothing at all you can do about it. Except in the rarest of circumstances, there's usually no room left for negotiation and bargaining. I've seen many lay off situations over my career as a developer and manager. I've seen only two cases where a person was able to hold onto their job once they were given the news.

If you are facing a situation where you have been told there is a performance issue, sometimes this is referred to as being put on a "performance improvement plan" (also known as a "PIP" or "a plan") but the exact terminology varies, you have a decision to make. You can:
1) Just quit immediately.
2) Take action to comply with that plan and get off the naughty list with an eye to keeping your job long term.
3) Take the immediate steps you need to take to remain employed **until** you can get your next position lined up.

I don't recommend the first choice. Don't let your emotions –
anger, hurt, betrayal – cause you to make a snap decision that
isn't in your best interest. It may feel better in the moment, but
emotion-driven decisions usually don't work out in the long
haul.

The second choice of doing whatever is needed to get back
into the good graces may seem attractive and it isn't entirely
crazy. However, even if you survive the performance plan, it's
really very difficult to fully recover from this. By the time a
manager takes this step, they have formed a picture of you in
their mind that is just hard to get past. I'm going to just be
transparent from a manager perspective and say that from a
regulatory, cost and general hassle standpoint, it is easier for a
large company to get underperforming employees to quit
rather than terminate them. The requirements of a
performance plan are often designed to lead employees to just
quit rather than stick it out. There are often a lot of
requirements related to dates, sending daily status, or other
friction-inducing hurdles. It's not always the case, but it
happens. It's not intended to be easy to survive a plan.

Because of that problem, a lot of career experts would say the
third choice is the way to go. Accept that the writing is on the
wall and if you haven't been sharpening your skills and
résumé, now is the time and get looking for what is next.

Being put on a performance plan should never be a true
surprise to you. You should be having regular one-on-one
discussions with your manager. You should be seeking
feedback from managers and peers – not to an obsessive or too
frequent degree, but you should take advantage of natural
opportunities like the end of a quarter, project endings or the
approach of performance review time at your company.

No matter the reason for the job loss, the best protection you have *always* is to be regularly sharpening your skills to stay current and keeping in touch with the market by interviewing regularly. A goal of at least one interview per quarter is reasonable. That's all true even if you are happy in your current job and have no intention to leave. It isn't always your choice. Don't be caught flat-footed and scrambling for a new position. There's an old (and true) saying that the best time to find a new job is when you already have one. In this process, you'll stay up to speed on how people are interviewing, what they care about and, importantly, how much they are willing to pay for it. I've had friends who literally had not interviewed for 10, 15 or even 20 years and are then faced with the need to find a new job and they have to deal with learning what that world looks like now while they are reeling from the emotional and financial impact of losing a job. Don't be that person. Think of it this way. If you are happily employed and you do a couple interviews for jobs and you completely flop because you weren't prepared for the questions, you've really lost nothing and learned a *lot* in return.

When you choose to move on

What if you aren't laid off, aren't on a performance plan, but you don't see a career trajectory for you? Maybe the organization is top-heavy with people in the positions ahead of you and they don't seem to be going anywhere to make room for you. Or maybe you just don't like the job, don't like the people, don't like the product or the business, or are just ready for new challenges and opportunities.

I'm just going to briefly restate what I said in the previous section about job loss. **Always be ready**. Always be developing skills, even if that means doing personal projects and spending some weekend time keeping up on technology trends and best practices. Keep that résumé up to date and looking the way people expect résumés to look right now (rather than five years ago when you last looked for a job). And interview. An interview isn't a marriage. It's just a casual date at a bar. You may not get an offer. If you do, you may not accept. That's all fine. Interviews and offers are the way the job market gives you important feedback.

And build your network, both in person as well as on social media tools like LinkedIn. Those connections are the strongest path to finding your next role. There is a huge difference between applying blindly on a job site and having a person who works at that company refer you internally. When people say, "I've submitted 300 job applications and résumés and haven't heard back from anyone!" Well, the data seem to show they are doing it wrong.

You should also ask your trusted friends in the industry to look at your résumé. What does it say to them? Ask them to send you theirs – especially if they have recently been through the hiring process. Style does matter with résumés – even in the 21st century. Similarly, you might ask what they think of your LinkedIn profile or other public presence you have on the web. There are people you can pay to help with all of this stuff. Almost always, I think that is unnecessary. You know people, probably quite a few of them. Some are more experienced at this than you, and *all* of them have opinions and fresh perspectives. Don't be afraid to ask them for some advice. And, what's more, if you have friends or even friends-of-friends who work at companies you are interested in, don't be afraid to ask them to make an internal referral for the positions where you think you are a great fit.

Now, go! Survive, thrive – and guide!

Phew! We've covered a lot of ground.

Returning a bit to where we started, yes, it would be a wonderful world if we could just write our code and close out our tasks and make steady progress in terms of salary and other rewards. Sadly, in my experience, and in the shared experiences of the dozens of engineers just like you who I interviewed for this book, it just doesn't quite work out that way.

However, nothing in this survival guide says you need to turn into a desperate political animal either. You don't need to hold other people back for you to get ahead. You don't need to create secret fiefdoms of information only you know. In fact, just the opposite path of understanding why you are doing what you are doing, helping other people hit their goals, and sharing information broadly is *the way*.

True, now and then, we still see people who seem to be succeeding by playing the villain, but it won't last. Even technical work is a *people business* and, unsurprisingly, people don't respond well to someone who treats them badly.

So, go on, nail your job, make a map, know your business, manage your brand and don't be annoying. Not only will you succeed, but you'll guide other great people along that path with you, too.

Reading list & bibliography

I've mentioned several books and sources, but I've been influenced by *many*. Some are more directly related to the work of a software engineer, but all can teach you how to thrive in large organizations. You may not see project management or innovation or psychology as your core job, but all of these apply to your overall success.

Berkun, Scott. *The Art of Project Management.* (O'Reilly Media, 2015)

Chartered Management Institute. *New Study: Bad managers and toxic work culture causing one in three staff to walk.* (CMI, October 16 2023). https://www.managers.org.uk/about-cmi/media-centre/press-releases/bad-managers-and-toxic-work-culture-causing-one-in-three-staff-to-walk/

Christensen, C. M. *The Innovator's Dilemma.* (Harvard Business Review Press, 2016)

Cloud, Henry. *Necessary Endings.* (Harper Collins, 2011)

Davis, Kathleen. *The Science of Miscommunication at Work.* (FastCompany December 5 2022) https://www.fastcompany.com/90818044/science-of-miscommunication-at-work

Deming, W. Edwards. *Out of the Crisis.* (Massachusetts Institute of Technology, Center for Advanced Engineering Study, 1982)

Gladwell, Malcolm. *The Tipping Point: How Little Things Can Make a Big Difference.* (Back Bay Books, 2002)

Graham, Paul. *Maker's Schedule, Manager's Schedule.* (PaulGraham.com, July 2009) https://paulgraham.com/makersschedule.html

Hammack, Bill. *The Things We Make.* (Sourcebooks, 2023

Lieby, Violet. *Worldwide Professional Developer Population of 24 Million Projected to Grow amid Shifting Geographical Concentrations.* (Evans Data Corporation, May 21 2019) https://evansdata.com/press/viewRelease.php?pressID =278

Lowisz, Steve. *Why the Sandwich Approach To Criticism Is Terrible Advice.* (Forbes, April 25 2022) https://www.forbes.com/sites/forbeshumanresourcesc ouncil/2022/04/25/why-the-sandwich-approach-to-criticism-is-terrible-advice/

Matyszewksi, Robert. *Advantages and Problems of Small Software Company.* (SoftwareHut Blog, May 12 2017) https://softwarehut.com/blog/it-outsourcing/advantages-and-problems-of-small-software-company

Schwarz, Roger. *The "Sandwich Approach" Undermines Your Feedback.* (Harvard Business Review, April 19 2013) https://hbr.org/2013/04/the-sandwich-approach-undermin

Shigeoka, Scott. *Seek: How Curiosity Can Transform Your Life and Change the World.* (Balance, November 14 2023)

Stocker, Gregg. *Deming and Lean.* (Lessons in Lean, November 25 2012) https://leadingtransformation.wordpress.com/2012/11 /25/deming-and-lean/

Tulip. *What are the Five Whys? A Tool For Root Cause Analysis.* (Tulip). https://tulip.co/glossary/five-whys/

Yeung, Andrew. *I got promoted quickly at companies like Meta and Google by following this career tip: 'Eat the frog'.* (Business Insider, January 3 2024) https://www.businessinsider.com/eat-the-frog-promotions-meta-google-2023-12

Acknowledgements

Many people have been incredibly helpful in the creation of this book.

At the risk of pandering a bit, I want to thank two managers I had early in my career when I, frankly, was a bit of a hothead. They taught me more than they'll probably ever realize. Ian Mercer, then president of Automap Inc. (which was later acquired by Microsoft) and Kurt von Nieda, my first manager at Microsoft. Thanks also to people those who managed the more mature and polished version of me. Especially David Markley, who was my manager at Amazon for just a short time but who made such an impact that I still follow him on LinkedIn for the leadership wisdom he shares and you should too. (https://www.linkedin.com/in/davidmarkley/). Indeed, thanks to all my other managers and leaders at Microsoft, Amazon, Twitch, Voicebox Technologies and Unity who gave me the opportunity to work on some really cool stuff with amazing teams. Sometimes *convincing* me I could do it when I didn't think I was ready.

Jason Smith, Sam Menekar, Craig Tullis – all valued former colleagues, incredibly knowledgeable developers, skilled engineering leaders and great friends who have helped me bounce ideas back and forth, reviewed various sections of this book when they were sometimes very raw ideas and never held back on what they really thought – which is exactly what I needed.

Derek Askham and Cody Beyers who provided insight into the what engineers and analysts at an earlier stage in their careers need to know right now. They are emblematic of emerging influencers in our craft.

Brad Hartman-Maloy and Kelley Price, SPHR, SHRM-SCP, both of whom I've had the pleasure of working with in the past as my counterparts in HR in a couple companies, and Larry Austin, SPHR, also an experienced HR pro and friend. They gave invaluable feedback and guidance on the section about working with HR – about which I am definitely NOT an expert, but, thankfully, they are.

Thanks to the dozens of people I won't name who sat for interviews, responded to surveys, and otherwise made sure this is a book for all of us, not just "Jon's book."

And finally, thanks to my wife, Lynnae, for decades of support and patience, and for at least pretending to be interested all these years when I talked about work, being my first reviewer of anything and always giving valuable perspective and insight – and lots of fun discussion about the Oxford comma.

Index

About the Author

Since his teen years, Jon Pulsipher has been in professional software roles ranging from coding, to developer relations, to program and engineering management in a variety of companies and teams of all sizes (but mostly on the bigger side), including a tiny one bought by a huge one. From boring business solutions to exciting gaming technology, he's probably worked on it. He currently lives in the Austin, Texas area, mentoring and advising developers and leaders of software development teams, writing, speaking and trying to remember all the Z-80 and 6502 assembly language he used to know when he was young and smart.

Jon's always happy to chat about pretty much anything. You can find him at

> Web: jonpulsipherbooks.com
> LinkedIn: linkedin.com/in/jon-pulsipher
> Facebook: Jon Pulsipher Books
> X/Twitter: @Jons_Books

If you found this book helpful, sharing your review is always appreciated.